Godless
Circumcisions

Godless Circumcisions

A Recollecting &

Re-membering of

Blackness, Queerness & Flows of Survivance

Tabias Olajuawon Wilson

The Griot's Pen

Print Edition, 2015

Printed in the United States of America

ISBN-13: 978-1519539960
ISBN-10: 1519539967

Tabias Olajuawon

The Griot's Pen
Washington, DC 20008

www.blaqueerflow.com

To my nephews and niece Daiveyon, Eli and Emani.

There are many frightening things in the world—things that might cause you to question the purpose of living, to wonder if life is worth the toil, if your life matters—but your self shall never be one of them. Your freedom lies in your ability to hold, love and believe yourself, truly. Become familiar with the whispers within your soul. Trust them. They know exactly who you are. When the scalpel comes to greet your spirit— with promises of wealth, acceptance and mobility—smile and kindly turn it away. Remain intact, because in the valley of your essence rests the secrets of the great forever.

Acknowledgements

I must begin by thanking my mothers, for without them, I would not have survived birth, survived this world or survived myself. Thank you to maternal mother, LaToya, for giving me life and teaching me that kindness can exist under the most horrid of circumstances. To Willa Mae Wilson, my GRAND mother, thank you for your everlasting faith in my ability and *need* to be me. You taught me to speak my mind, trained me to speak my truth, and implored me to be myself. I will love you forever and ever and always. To LaCretia Grant, my aunty-momma-cuz, for holding me in the still of the night and relighting the fire in my spirit to be excellent, to love freely and live fully.

To my dear friends Rashad Malik Davis, of RAMalik Illustrations, Sophia Wright and Cydia Flowers for supporting me in the beginning with your creations of the cover, graphic and interior designs, respectively. Your support was the initial vote of confidence. I hope that you are as proud of this project as I am.

To my intellectual caregivers Drs. Sabina Vaught, Karen G. Gould and Christina Sharpe: it took your village and I rise from the bridge you built. To the late Brandon William Lacy-Campos, I miss you daily and remain inspired by your love-labor. To Haywood Perry, the one and only, for midwifing this idea and holding my hand and heart much long than I deserved.

To Hari Ziyad, my writing partner & soul brother for being the best gift of 2015. To Jonathan J. Moore, Delia Younge, Mauricio Torres and Venus Selenite—the original and founding members of the BlaQueerFlow family—for pushing me to write with fire and creating a space where my words, my spirit, my *me* could be seen, re-membered and collected yet again. To Mark Andrew Garner, seven years later, we have kept our word! To Francisco Luis White for their continued challenge of everything I have professed or endeavored to be and a love that knows few bounds. To Kiese

Laymon, John Stevenson and Darnell Moore for their continued amplification of my voice, my thoughts and my culture-work. To Michael Shoop, for introducing me to a love pure and true and for reminding me how to give and receive love: it appears white boys have soul, too :).

To Taurean McCrea for growing with me, humoring my rants and providing a resting and redemption space for a weary soul. To Briahna Logan, LaCole Spraggins, Monique Peterkin, Shaneka McKellar, Jameelah Morris, Valecia Battle, Stanton Burke, Charles Pierre, Akasha Camille and Professor Harold McDougall for allowing me to remain whole, conscious woke' during this journal called law school.

To my Harlem/Miami students, for foreshadowing the beauty and promise of a new and empowered black and brown generation. To Jerry Mitchell, my oldest and truest friend, this is for us. To Logan Cotton, Chad Davis & Eli Day: my straight calvary, confidants and brothers for always keeping me grounded and whole.

To Durand Bernarr—the first to give me permission to be so black, so queer and magically divine, I thank you. To Amir Dixon, Corey Yarborough, Quincey Roberts, Gabriel Maldonado, Guy Anthony, Justin Rush, Yolo Akili, Michael Webb, Blake Rowley, Elvin Fontana-Martinez, Noel Gordon, Brandon Anderson, Micky Bee, Travis Wise, Perre Shelton, AJ King, Matthew Rodriguez, Richard Pittman, Jamal T. Lewis, Martez Smith, Denzell Cammon, Damone Williams, Joshua Allen, Keith Jones, Marcus Lee, Romeo Jackson, Kenneth O'Veal, Brandon Smith, Shikeith Niree, Tiq Milan, Dean Richards, Carlos Harris, Brandon Smith, Fernando Gomez, Jason Michael, Jihad Broussard, Miles Hector, Terry Jones, Saeed Jones and Christopher Barnhill for living, loving and creating in a way that continually unchains the bodies, minds and souls of BlaQueer children and growin' folk across the globe. You are magic. The list goes on and on, from the fresh eyes editing this page, to the loyal readers and critics of BlaQueerFlow: The Griots' Pen, and those that provide loving sustenance across the cosmic spectrum: thank you all. This is our creation. This is for you.

CONTENT

Acknowledgements

Introduction
Cultural Circumcisions & Other Mortal Wounds (1)

A Love Letter To My Black, Queer Brothers *(3)*

Real Words For Real People (7)

Poetry
Attempts to Be Articulate (12)

Quotes & Affirmations
A Litany for Survival

Prose
Flesh, Bones & Intellect

INTRODUCTION

Cultural Circumcisions & Other Mortal Wounds

"It is a peculiar sensation, this double-consciousness, this sense of always look-
ing at one's self through the eyes of others, of measuring one's soul by the tape of
a world that looks on in amused contempt and pity."

-W.E.B Du Bois

"So, in my mind I'm tusslin'
Back and forth 'tween here and hustlin'
I don't wanna time travel no more
I wanna be here, I'm thinking.."

-Erykah Badu, Window Seat

We were born whole, announcing our presence as we emerged
from the flesh of our mothers with grand aplomb, we were whole. There
was nothing missing. Even then, we knew who and where we were. We
knew how and when to breathe. Our heart had long began beating on its
own, paying no mind to the rhyme and reason of the beating hearts around
it. We knew our nakedness and had no shame, because we were whole.
Nothing was missing. There was no good hair, or bad hair, if any at all.
Our skin was neither too dark, nor too light, too brown or too white, we
were whole. Nothing was missing. We came into this world complete and
ready to continue living. Our spirits were on a mission to continue a cycle
of learning and becoming that which they'd always longed for--oneness--

unity with the Cosmos, or the Great Creator, Energy, or Goddess, The One Who Birthed Us All. We were born ready, until they brought out the scalpel.

The bleeding continues into adulthood--the wound unable to cauterize--as the silent sickness of performativity consumes us. We are unable to be fully present, fully us, whole, anywhere. We exist only in our separate spheres: race, gender, class, profession, religion, sexuality, sex, family, friend, employer, neighbor, caregiver, citizen or resident. I yearn to break free from these neoliberal, Godless Circumcisions, loving myself to Cosmic Reconciliations, reuniting with that which was cleaved at birth. This is my journey: a litany for survival.

A Love Letter To My Black, Queer Brothers

"This is for my brothers who dare to love

other brothers in a revolutionary way."

Writing to you is an exercise in self-love and holistic restoration. I am called to reckon with the promise of my future, the depths of my own greatness, accessed and denied. You are the world. It has been said that black is the absence of light, ain't it funny how they always get that wrong? The tea is, blackness is the essence of creation, a potpourri of the creative ingredients of existence. Blackness, unbought, unbossed and un-restrained is the building block of color and from its presence, our presence, your presence, derives all things.

"This is for the man-child, always man, sometimes child, because duality is how we make it to tomorrow."

My thoughts drift to you often, my BlaQueer brothers. Flesh deep, varied and enduring as that of the earth on which we stand. Arms strong and versatile enough to hold masculinities, femininities and the journey of ancestors close. You are rhythmic, moving through the compounded obstacles of society step-by-step, death-dropping over stigma, tossing shade to the bright lights of white supremacy and sashaying truths of our over-comings through your very existences.

"This is for limp wrist warriors, full of sugar, dripping honey and snatching the creative energy of the cosmos."

You are a soul ballad; stitching together the complex realities of our fraught existences with an in-articulable presence that commands and requires respect, resolve and r/evolution. You are a Cosmos; within you exists a constellation of brilliant expressions of perfect imperfections.

"This is for the choir boys, ministers, and ushers praying, hoping and calling for Heaven—here and now—who refuses to divide black from queer, queer from male and Him into itty, bitty, homophobic bite-size pieces.."

You are queer, trans, gay, bi, and same-gender-loving. You are father, son, brother, uncle, cousin, and homie. You are truth-seeker, griot, artist, scholar, activist, organizer, writer, singer, designer, athlete, lawyer, educator, trend-setter, and him. You are him. He who is sensitive yet indestructible, authentic yet ever-evolving, sexually breathtaking and intellectually stupefying.

"This is for the Survivors, fighting a war within, against cells unrelenting, brothers not-repenting and community to afraid to love and live in the presence of HIV."

Simultaneously existing within and outside imputed markers and communities of race, gender, and sexuality, we trek on the path of our forefathers. We speak with the urgency of Malcolm, the insight of Baldwin and the truth Essex. We live with the fearlessness, strategic, acuity of Joseph

Beam and Bayard Rustin; navigating the world with our eyes on holistic, comprehensive justice. We create and we love, with the fire and passion of Ru, Langston and Rotimi Fani-Kayode. From their shoulders and their pathways we are called and empowered to be all that we are; realizing and releasing the divine nature of our BlaQueerness in honor of the crowns of our lineage, the proof of present and the hope of our progeny. From trans-misogyny to police violence, from femme-phobia to HIV criminalization, from poverty to sex-shaming: we are all we need to thrive. Indeed, we are all we've ever had.

Quotations are from the poem "This Is For You" co-written with Amir Dixon. This originally appeared in MusedMagOnline.

Real Words For Real People

Definitions: Real Words For Real People

Many of the words used in this collection are above my pay-grade and are not the not words, general phrases or ways in which my folks—working-class folks, folks of color, black folks, queer folks—would use to describe systems of power, practices of love or, as we say back home, the way things are/is/oughtta' be. However, some of the issues presented in this book were always known back home—here, now and then—but they didn't have names to them, folks couldn't put their finger on them or perhaps, they were things not best said in polite company or outside one's own head. For that reason, there are quite a few academic, ten-dollar words, that I'm going to break down into my folk's terms. This is not your everyday dictionary. No, it is a thesaurus/dictionary blend in a language that matters to my folks. You'll see few cites here, because this isn't for the academy.

1. **Cisgender**: When your perception of your gender, male/female, agrees with the sex you were assigned at birth.

2. **Patriarchy**: A system of society, government, culture and power distribution where men wield inequitable, unnatural amounts of power, influence and violence while women (and often children) are largely excluded from such freedom. Patriarchy is when men are assumed to be born leaders, heads of households, presidents and women are assumed, persuaded and encourage to follow, submit, keep quiet or bitch and work for less money on the dollar. It is a system where the wants, desires, needs, expertise, feelings, intelligence and humanity of women-folk is discounted or used largely in service of the man.

3. **Hetero**: Refers to heterosexual.

4. **Cisheteropatriarchy**: A system of patriarchy where cisgender men wield power and have access to humanity at inequitable rates as stated in #2. However, this definition implicitly mentions—by using cis—the

plight of non-cis peoples (queer peoples, trans* folks, femme men, masculine women, GNC folk).

5. **Sex**: These are the physical characteristics assigned at birth—chromosomes, internal reproductive structures, external genitalia—that correlate to the binary categories of male and female.

6. **Gender**: Socially constructed or given roles, behaviors, activities, and attributes that society considers appropriate for men and women. Gender is performed. It is not biological, but instead a collection of meanings and beliefs we have constructed to organize and categorize people, power and self. There are many genders in the world beyond the binary man/woman. There are also people who defy the gender binary of man/woman and identify as simply their name or as Gender-Non-Conforming (GNC). There are also many people in the world who identify Transgender (Trans*); many of which identify as male, female, transmale, transfemale, GNC or simply Trans*. There are personal, cultural and political reasons that each of choose to perform—or rebel against—particular genders. There is no answer that fits each person. To begin the process of understanding gender, you should ask yourself, what is a woman/man? Are these things real? What makes them real? Are there accomplishments, emotions, truths, loyalties, friendships, violence, relationships, spiritual heights or even deaths you cannot experience because you're a man, a woman, Trans*, neither? Did the universe make you incomplete, or superior? If so, why? If not, why not? How much more human is one person over the other if we all bleed red blood and have numbered days and timeless souls?

7. **Feminism**: Famously described by bell hooks as "a movement to end sexism, sexist exploitation, and oppression."[1] Others would not that it is a belief system, a practice and a way of living life shared by anyone

---

[1] hooks, b. (2000). Feminism is for everybody: Passionate politics. Pluto Press.

who cares about freedom of self and others (men, that means you too!).

8. **Misogynoir**: The live, active and critical Facebook Group "Unpacking Misogynoir" describes it as: "a term originally coined by Dr. Moya Bailey (formerly of the Crunk Feminist Collective), which describes the unique and specific ways that Black women have been dehumanized throughout history, and in our contemporary societies. Misogynoir is a unique combination of woman hate, also known as misogyny, and anti-Blackness, the specific dehumanization and negation of Black people."[2]

9. **Race**: Race is often defined as a category resulting from one's phenotypical characteristis: skin color, hair texture and bone structure. However, it is more accurately explained a cultural and systemic reaction to —and mystical belief in the reality of—these markers of surface-level difference. Race is a stand-in for categories, stereotypes, meanings, assumptions and socioeconomic and legal consequences placed on individuals and groups by societies, communities, families and self. Examples include, to varying levels of agreement, Black, White, Asian, Indigenous/First Nation/Native and sometimes Latino and Mixed-Race in the Unted States. This system of categorization is clearly flawed, limited and human-made.

10. **Ethnicity**: Is often understood as race+geography+culture (and sometimes religion). The difference here is both small and large. Think: Black (race) vs African-American (ethnicity). It's not simply about the way you look, but where your people come from. Interestingly, Latinx (Latina/o*) folks are often characterized as an ethnicity rather than a race. There are many reasons for this, that I won't get into here, but I will remind you that there are black latinos (AfroLatinos), white-latinos and so on. It's quite uncomfortable writing this, because as you can see, it's as if someone's race modifies or conditions their ethnicity.

---

[2] Unpacking Misogynoir (2016). About Me Section. https://www.facebook.com/groups/937657119578763/ Accessed: 1/4/16.

Please Note: Mexican is not a race. It is a nationality. It is a nation of millions of folks with beating hearts, loving families and American-created problems.

11. **White Supremacy**: An ideological brand of racism that centers white people, and whiteness, as *the* humans in society; whereby every other group and type of person is inferior. It is also a practice and a system; whereby white culture, white enjoyment, white property, economic, legal, political, sexual and religions interests and norms are protected by law, policing and the practice of (mis)education. White supremacy is practiced by white people, black people, latinx folks, asian people, indigenous people, mixed-raced folks and people of all stripes. Black folks know this truth from the phrase "If you're white you're right." While that may not be 100% true in all circumstance, you wager that in court, when facing police or anyone with authority (teacher, landlord, employer) that if you practice white culture, your at least always *more right* than if you were being yourself..which may mean a white person who doesn't drink the kool-aid, or a black person just being themselves.

12. **Queer**: A political practice, a movement, an ideology that seeks to reimagine and deconstruct notions of normalized violence. It is the strange commitment to the idea that folks born free should live free, with excellent food, ideas and insurmountable love at their disposal. Being queer is not simply about who you fuck, or how you fuck, but also why you fuck and in what world you choose to live, what world you choose to maintain or co-create. Queerness is more than sexual or gender performance. It is the strange commitment to the idea that folks born free should live free, with excellent food, ideas and insurmountable love at their disposal.

13. **Intersectionality/Compoundedness**: These terms, by Kimberle Crenshaw, speak to the reality of living. They note the reality and lived effects of the overlapping, compounding and intersecting social identities and related systems of oppression, domination or discrimination. The theory notes that one is never just black, or just woman, or just

10

poor or just 53; instead it posits that age, race, gender, sexuality, class, sex, education level, (dis)ability, nationality, language, ethnicity all occur in the same bodies at the same time. Therefore when we speak about issues, say, violence in black and brown communities, we cannot simply be speaking about race but we must also note that these issues are the results of systems that make and create race, as well as class, as well as gender and in-access to certain educations for people different spaces, at certain ages. In short, our problems are systemic, multifaceted and so are the struggles, identities, beauties and stories of our lives. Humans are as complex as the worlds we live in.

14. **BlaQueer**: Black folks who refuse to have their blackness or queerness dominate over the other but instead let each flow as naturally as the melanin that colors our skin.

15. **Humanization**: The process of becoming, understanding oneself and being seen and received as human.

POETRY

Attempts to be articulate

I Don't Want To Be Scene

I'm not a scene boy,

Never have been.

My worth and value have never been

tied to visibility

being here nor there,

running back and forth announcing

my relevance to the ambivalence of other

folks trying to be seen

scene

And home in that space of flashing lights

and rallies thundering with empty applause,

hoping and praying for a rapture that might capture a moment in time

when self is relevant to self, or others

To capture a moment when hair, lips, brows and biceps are on fleek and

prepped for the performance

Pretty Hurts, Petty Burns, The Scene Erases

I've never wanted to be scene, being black, and queer, and somewhere be-
yond masculinity, nestled in proud, black poverty. Proud like black folks
in lawn chairs barbecuing meats & meets white folks would never eat or
greet, because they cause sudden death, yet smiling all the while because
you can at least afford that, performance, in the scene and gaze of white
ambivalence and black yearning. Fuck dying. We all die.

I want to be felt–soul nuzzled against, with, inside, adjacent to soul(s).
Studying communal war, no more.

Heard–the way my voice sounds in my head, no longer strangled or man-
gled by misinterpretations of my timbre and essence

Re-membered–body, mind psyche reconstituted as the spirit sent down
from the Cosmos and the ancestors

Still–no stages, movements or performatives. A self no longer engaged in
a daily practice of suicide.

I pray for the mimes of the unseen scene. I hope their souls from freedom
in being heard. I pray for an ancestral rapture, coming to sweep us togeth-

er into a liberatory collision where I feel you, and you feel seen and the spectacle of our homelessness is no more.

Photos, followers and the like have never healed a broken, black heart.

Satin Men

Men of the sheets beckon

with eyes that seem to

look into your soul

and pull at the heat of your

thighs, wider and wetter still

than the river Euphrates

supplying fuel to implanted thoughts

broken dams and walls of resistance

long-since held still by an insistence

on purity, security and (be)longing

to someone who resides in your heart, spirit

household. But those damn men of the sheets

know how to remind of you the feeling when flesh collides

with familiar and unfamiliar collisions of epidermal matter,

it matters not, then, whether s/z/he will stay in the morning

but whether you or not you can last as long as you remember

when your lips start to quiver

and your hips are no longer held firm

by your will power but the sheer power

of his entry

will you moan

in the sweet

sweat of satisfaction

or awaken

in tears of silent,

emptiness

in the mourning?

A Quick Blunt

Fresh off of a low tide I
rolled in the presence of your warm
thickness. Tightly packaged, reaching heights
I'd last seen in the rolling hills of home
long forgotten. Lips dark from loving,
licking and sealing the gift of being lifted.
I knew it. I knew I wanted you. But one puff is enough
for a brother to choke, or be stoned or to hunger for
something more fulfilling that you,
or I,
may not have at our disposal. May not be
able to afford to give that which is desired and I'd be

stuck.

faded.

frozen.

Soul growling with munchies because I tasted the blunt truth

of your essence but you couldn't give me the depths of your

spirit. I wouldn't hear it. Couldn't handle the

throat chop of love,

so fuck it.

Give me a quick blunt, sealed with the sweetness

of your full lips. So I can soar high and

forget these scars of unrequited affections.

The Cloak of Invisibility

It gives
and it takes.
It is familiar. I was born into it,
in a sense.
When I was born, the world didn't
see the possibilities of me
thriving
here and black and queer
with aplomb and no humility.
Screaming black babies,
hollering black children,
knowing,
seeing,
being something
other than dead
or living to serve others
and be freely othered,
visibly
home is where the hatred is
for far too many
where our intellect is hypervisible
and our blackness seems to escape
us with the need to be beaten
back in lest we begin to think
we are white
and (more) right

than those around us
Funny how intellect
can be raced and erased
from the blackened mind
reconstruction didn't
reroute or recoup neurons
affected by the lash of white,
class, sexual, color'd
supremacies.
Some of don it by choice,
the cloak,
some of us are chafed by the
zipper
None of us wear it
freely.
It wears us.
Only to be noted when we
are out of place/s
to hide
is impossible
a dream deferred
or perhaps preferred
by black folk
burned by light
of day
truth
and existence in
the mirror

no one
is
unseen.

There Is No Armor In Suits

There is no armor

in suits or ties,

they will not protect

you from the lies of

distance from blackness

and white rage through

masking performances of respectability

No,

death does not reside

in sweet tea and hoodies

and dialects as long

and black

as locs on the back

Rastafarian adherents.

There is no safety in proper

speech,

it will not protect from the systemic leach

that feeds on your essence,

leaving you with a shell

of blackness

cowering in shadows of

professionalism where only

your resume shines brightly

telling stories of jobs

and degrees you've held

and been cut through

pounds of flesh never

bled so hard

in silence

if only there were armor

in suits

and ties

and lovers

and guys that thought

they could protect by being

new and black

and shiny

new blacks.

No.

Disarming yourself of blackness

will you leave you naked in the

frigid grip of loneliness and white supremacy

burning your spirit cold

like fingers left

out of gloves

in a Boston

Snowmeggond.

There is no armor

for those who place

the scalpel

on their

own flesh

and that of those

born whole

and

black

and loving. There is no

armor in suits, just bodies

with ill-fitting designs

that mangle and constrain

the brains of peoples

once free

once one

once home,

in no need of armor

or suits.

More lies I swallow

as I knot my tie.

It's Coming For You: The Noose That Stole Our Sister, Sandra

We,

black folk,

all know the feeling

of the noose.

We gasp for air

when we see them roll

by with badges,

or in large groups.

We know in any second,

our access to air,

the power to breathe

freely might just be cut off.

We feel it in the classrooms too.

If we speak too passionately

we will be disciplined

and dismissed

as a scourge and true representative

of our race.

If we speak plainly,

we are noted as stupid,

rotten fruits of so-called affirmative actions.

The noose grows tighter.

We

feel

it.

We feel it when

our children and

siblings are out at night

and the news casually

mentions the death

–not murder–

of black boys and girls,

and we pray

"not ours."

Blisters

on

our

necks.

We

can't

breathe.

Election season comes around.

They tell us

#BlackLivesMatter,

to their pocketbooks

and campaign prospects.

Sure,

we know,

black folks built the White House,

and only black death

can buy it back.

The noose lifts us off our feet.

Barack says

"pull up your pants."

Hillary chuckles

and says "all lives matter"

before she moves on

to press a

"black for hillary sticker on your heart.

O'Malley smiles

and reminisces on "good ole days

in Baltimore" when

your blocks burned.

Sanders speaks…

of "billionaires,

crooked capitalism

and King"

he sees your pockets

have holes, but not your hands

sweaty,

on the noose.

Sandra fought for you,

while Rachel imitated you.

Sandra Bland.

#SayHerName

She was Harriet.

She was Assata.

She was Malcolm.

She was Angela.

She

is

dead

and you're still hanging.
Will you die peacefully?
or cut down this tree
powered
by black bloodletting?
and demonstrate
the essence of blackness unbound,
unbought

29

and unlynched?

Walk with me, family

and let us honor the blood of our

sojourning sister.

Breaking Roots

The breakage begins at the extremities

but always finds its way to the roots

to the heart

of the host

showing its disrespect for the

work of the housekeeper

s/he that did their best

to nurture

a space called

home.

Life Among The Undead

I cannot explain why

or how I continue to place myself

on the auction block,

to be poked,

prodded,

groped and enjoyed

and

for a moment,

held

by these men of violent persuasions

that want nothing more than to

use me

for their temporary empowerment. They

drink from my essence

like a fraternity of

JV Dracula's clinging to the veins

of the unwilling for another chance at eternal

existence as the undead.

Blood Sport

Love Sport

Power Lusts.

They are not living,

yet I cannot die.

I subsist in a prison of my own construction,

testing the bounds of my humanity,

the power of the aorta

to continue to pump

enough

life force

to remain alive

while becoming intimate with death's

shadows.

It would be more sad,

perhaps,

If i were helpless

but the flow of my own blood

was at once cathartic,

an ancient ritual of bloodletting

freeing me from my weaker self

positioning me as the fuel of another's

survival,

a life force,

sustaining ecosystems

flawlessly.

Even the Earth has her limits,

as I arise,

closing the holes of my veins

I marvel at my own fuckery,

the hubris,

the waste,

the pieces of my

brilliance,

time,

love given to boys

who became drunk at the sight of me

never taking in my true image

or essence

or divinity.

I almost killed myself,

trying to live among them.

As We Lay

I Pray For A Rapture

As we lay

a tear flees each of my eyes

in a cold, prideful

defeat

with each caress of his

breathe against the small

of my

neck. He sleeps

peacefully nuzzled up

against me.

Drawing strength from my consistent,

unwavering love and

support and super-humanity.

As we lay,

I grow closer to

death and I

hope I may soon meet my

maker in a rapture of the over-lovers.

Those of us, who love freely and loudly

while wasting away in silence, restrained

and elegant.

Because I can no longer

fight the sadist within

that controls the functions of my veins,

nor the can I muster the strength to challenge the onslaught

of empty men with open hands,

barren hearts,

hollow spirits and

parasitic,

genocidal ethics of

survival.

As we lay,

I pray for his death

and mine

and yours.

Because we all deserve to live,

someday.

You're Asking Me of Freedom?
Black Talks Back

It's cruel,

to ask us what

freedom

looks like

When you,

and your forefathers

have hid it for years.

Criminalized it's

presence

in our own American Day Dreams,

turned into nightmares

for fear that

freedom

may be another

cruel

trick of the master's

dynastic

rule of terrorists

trip wires.

It's cruel,

to ask us of

freedom,

when tongues are lashed for its

pronunciation

in

black

brown

queer

trans

poor

and disabled

mouths..

sending shivers

through your

soul.

So you take ours,

suckling

to feel

free and

strong again,

because redemption rests in the

inheritance of the meek.

Freedom is

a cruel

bait to the gates

of the dead

We disavow your

freedom

and speak of

Liberation

                                                                    Autonomy

                                        Love

            Healing.

Absence from racist mythologies.

Flows of blackness

unhindered by white

dams

Flowing,

deeper than rivers of psycho-analytic thought

Deeper,

than the bosom of entrapped

bodies in musty ships

whipped through

the Atlantic

in chains

of false hope.

We survived that, too.

Reclaimed the passage as

Homeschooled tutorial

have lost some,

but hold them close

in memorial

we speak their names

Trayvon Martin.

Sandra Bland.

Tamir Rice.

Renisha McBride.

Jordan Davis.

Tanisha Anderson.

Jamar Clark

Janisha Fonville

Eric Garner

Natasha McKenna

Ezell Ford

Sherese Francis

Walter Scott

Kendra James

Freddie Gray

Still deeper,

Blackness flows from the core of Earth,

to the cover of the flesh

and the heart of the

Cosmos,

Adorned with shooting stars

Undettered by the scars

Of being black, gifted

And whole in Amerikka.

To ask us of freedom is cruel

and curious

Like breaking a man's jaw

And asking why his teeth don't stand erect.

We speak of liberation

from the menace of spec

and the prison of spectacle

We seek to rest

in the absence of white indifference,

And Other Facebook filters,

Unassigned to violences

On bodies of color,

That our society cosigns,

for cheap oil,

capitalisms

and others ways to make cents

off of bodies born free

that we refuse to let be,

but here's the key.

we will be free from

black death,

Islamaphobic bombings,

Native genocides,

As family, we will decide

The unbought won't plead for freedom

We burn,

we birth

we build

for

Liberation.

Your fear is logical.

Honey, Love & Blackness

Oh shug!

My love is vast as the ocean is deep,

But your arms don't seem strong enough to sail my waves.

Honey-chile!

This lovin is as sweet and quenching as big momma's good Sunday tea on

a thick summer eve'nin

But you don't have a taste for the gifts of love.

Baby boy!

I could rock your world with the flick of my wrist

But the quakes & shivers would destroy your foundation.

Bae,

I've been waiting for you to sip from the chalice

of my love.

But your mind is trained on thots

and I'm vast,

a child of the BlaQueer mystique

an heir of the Cosmos.

So I watch and wait,

til time stops speaking and

you awaken

to us.

To kiss

and say

I'm home.

Good Morning.

Black or Brown or Colored, Boy?

That black boy,

butter

brown skin,

stuffed pink lips

and coiffed high top

fade,

line on fleek.

He rides

on a bright white

bike with two

tiny wheels through

the streets of Capetown.

I wonder,

colored boy,

Do you see your blackness?

Fucking Blackness: Explosions, Invasions & Predatory Niggas

Click, Smile, Click, Smile, Giggle,

I had smiled, at first

when I saw the children

running toward me with toothy grins

on mahogany brown faces, bearing hope of a

tomorrow I dreamt of for them but feared in the depths of

my suicidal, capitalistic, humanist heart would never come true.

We stood there as dream thieves catchers, so-called Social Engineers

from Amerikkka, positioning ourselves as the black embodiment of clas-

sist

bullshit, force-fed hot down the psyche of young black girls that knew

better than us

about the cost of being mahogany black, gifted and poor

gifted with IQ's higher than bill gates, warren buffet or whatever other capitalist jockeying WP you can find in the billionaire-class of modern slaveholders.

Shit was real,

I tasted the dust, dirt and yes, the bones (of a dog) in Capetown in what used to be designated black district. It's ain't shit different,

it's a hood with a different tongue,

same skin,

black-brown, blue-black, high yella, black niggas

hungry and starving

but making due like only

blue-black, black-brown, high yella, black niggas

can do.

Make believing like only high yella, mahogany brown, blue-black, black children niggas

can do.

Shit turned my stomach.

Na, shit took my stomach, flipped it upside down and churned

it like butter in big mommas wooden bin.

It wasn't the poverty that killed me, tho

that shit cut. It wasn't the stench of septic tanks

or the white folks touring black spaces to exorcise white guilt

on black faces or white prerogatives in black cunts and asses

that shit stank, the festering sore of white supremacy on flesh so beautiful

and strong,

was,

sickening but it wasn't that.

Na, it was the fucking clicking. The clicking and the giggling. The click-

ing, the giggling, the petting zoo performed, orchestrated, and demanded

of black people by black people from historically black institutions in a

black nation to further their white supremacist understanding of a white

supremacist world and legal framework so that they might engineer a way

to join a system of plundering black(er) bodies with coin,

culture and

a vengeance.

They clicked that fucking camera like they were

hoping to click themselves away from the space and time

where these struggling black folks

looked like them

shared they blood

and knew them.

They clicked distance.

They giggled because they had found a way to be comfortable

being uncomfortable as the bastard offspring of the

of white, heterosexist, patriarchal, capitalism that require the souls

and flesh of their kin for fuel

and their skin for tools

to make it more palatable

because "Nigga we made it"

don't mean shit, without the crumbs

and accoutrements of the master.

That fucking clicking.

Stealing images of children playing in dirt roads

besides the toothie skulls of dead dogs

that had long since departed..

the invitation of homes, interrupting struggling mothers

preparing meager meals for children and that fucking

click, smile, giggle

Shit was killing me. I sat outside and felt dirty. Even as

the mothers smiled and the children waved,

feigning happiness and hospitality.

Shit maybe it was real.

The poor are the realest, illest, gifters of all that they/we have.

But this shit was sinister. It stank. It churned my soul. It was clear that

they were being paid,

by a black tour-guide company,

and our enjoyment, delight and eroticization of their pain

was the only way African black folk

could access the gaze of black African-America niggas,

with pockets of coin, degrees on fleek and eye on master's

53

mansion, whip and leash.

So they gave us pleasure,

they stroked us slow,

often,

gentle

then hard..

because maybe if we busted

the violence porn,

might just be enough

to make us family.

Capetown: The Men 'Round Here

Family,

I know they are family,

Brothers even,

but we are distant

distinct

with a kindred flesh.

Perhaps our father covered

the continent like a strong

gust of blackness.

My brothers here are

distinct.

Their walk does

not command the world

to hum and recall the

rhythm of their step

nor does their face

speak of a dual sweetness

and onyx sword but

instead they disarm with

wide, bright smiles that seem

permanent and routinely

ends the callousness of hearts long

rubbed raw and through by truths of

white supremacist,

capitalistic,

cisheteropatriachal

fuckery.

Small waists with thick hips

that are accustomed to carrying and

bearing the loads of

apartheid.

Bulges full of flesh that

snake down legs causing

the hips and lips of the casual voyeur

to tremble

with fear, lust and delight for

the night that s/he/they too

may taste the

fruit of the

motherland's

first born.

They stand with a gentle pride. Knowing

something of the world,

something of you,

that cannot

be

said

in polite company.

True that their nation

is recovering from the prison of whiteness but

truer still, that we are

the bastard children of white

violence and the motherland's blood-stained gate.

Rude,

true

regal. But

taken gently under the guidance of two

large, black-bright and watchful

eyes.

My God!

The way they

shine!

The South African

men.

Brothers.

Family.

How I've silently longed

for a loving reunion.

A Blue-Black Tulip Speaks of Blooming

I open,

like a tulip making her

annual rise from the mud. I come

from the thick of it. Thick, wet, lands

that know of stories. More than his/herstories, yes. Truths

about the thickness, the place on which our realities spring and stand

I come from there. A child of the cosmos,

searching for the sun

as I push,

out

of the mud,

that thickness, that if not tilled properly

will cause certain asphyxiation. Weaker flowers

have died, daily, annually..but always before flowering.

I've seen roses, supported by the bush, fall to the wayside due to the

thickness.

Well, perhaps it wasn't about the thickness at all, not about their momma

or poppa

flowers pruning or the cutting edges. No, it surely was not about

the way they presented themselves before being plucked,

depetaled and deflowered. For some flowers, for most flowers,

our lives are governed by the wind,

so we relish the time we have out of the thickness,

being smiled upon by the sun

before we are plucked

by viewers that know

not our given names

they know me as

the tulip

the bright one

he who has emerged

unscathed.

But I'm Tabias

cut below and through my petals

by pluckers wishing to take me too

soon,

saved by my mothers,

sisters,

uncles

and grandmothers from

deaths known to flowers like

me, growing from stone and concrete

hiding behind those seen as weeds

for our protection,

hoping to defeat detection

of our value

to the pluckers

to our people

as more than flowers

more than tulips

as the,

living.

DayDreams & The Prison of Productivity

Deadlines. Rubrics. Deadlines. Evaluations. Publications. Deadlines. Speeches. Panels. Conference Calls. Deadlines. MOU. Coffee. (Working) Lunch. Deadlines. Eat. Pray. Love-ish. Deadlines. Rush. Run. Exercise. Cry (On Time). Deadlines. Dead. Lines. Death Lines. Flat Line.

I have a dream that one day, people will be judged not by the quantity of their production but the quality of their existence(s).

Dream Deferred. Like a tulip in the winter. Frozen. Undead. Not quite

living.

I have a dream that one day, proclamations of excellence will surrender the throne of authenticity and prestige to excellence embodied by acts of love, humanity, brilliance and creativity.

But they don't have no awards for that..trophies..

Our bodies have been

transformed.

Once temples, holy tabernacles

of the divine embodied

at home

in our flesh…

now simple mills for production

of things made of lesser

concoctions of the cosmos

to give us

value to ourselves

for others

for ourselves

because we no longer know

the beauty

the time

the story

the moment

the divine

the perfect-imperfections of

our

selves.

Caitlyn's Calvary: The Gaze, The gays & Whiteness on Fleek

No cis person can articulate the internal traumas

of a person in transition

whether physically or internally

because the pain and societal

dismemberment of existing

in a space where your gender performance and identity

are read as misplaced because your soul won't confirm

or conform

to society's rules of gender-sexual circumcisions required for a passport

to humanity. Cis folks, my folks, these folks and many queer folks will

never know the pain of the scalpel unraveling, undoing, re-pasting, with-

out consent

notions of them, theirs, her, he, zhe, they...

because we–the gender conformers–have always been in line with the bio-

logical and sociological unholy union between genders, sex, sexuality, re-

alities, performances, identities and belonging

Despite the fact that we stay longing

for a moment of communion with our real selves

ourselves

our

selves

yet we succumb to fear of self and become

sociopolitical surgeons

not doctors

just performers of surgeries on the bodies

of the othered,

hoping to be seen and perceived as normal,

beautiful

supreme.

We are emotional and psychological terrorists,

vain,

65

coloring ourselves as the conscious and concerned while

simultaneously dismembering trans*gressors of hegemonic

gender divisions,

segregations

apartheids.

But Caitlyn has a cavalry.

Whiteness comes and cleans sociocultural

stains of difference,

it disinfects the blood let from the

scalpel and allows

the flesh to instead to become a cloth,

a cleaning

cloaking

cloth

that leaves its covering of whiteness

remaining pristine as a proof

of its universal powers of redemption,

its station as savior

and it's function of black

brown

color'd

erasures.

Caitlyn's Calvary comes in full force and

not all of her soldiers are born white

or right

of queer.

Many are black with white swords,

supremacist smiles and wintry-cold eyes

that disallow them to see trans* folk of color

as human

at all

ever.

They gays of Caitlyn's calvary note their own redemption

in their ability to receiver her as human,

this time,

as if this recognition erases their erasure

of black & brown trans* flesh

gnashed

slashed

strangled

in their presence

by their essence

and investments

in gender-normativity as an innate proclivity in all who deserve to live

unbought

unbossed

and unkilled. Black gays,

black gaze, celebrating Caitlyn in morning

but have no time for mourning their sistahs:

Lamia Beard

68

Taja Dajesus

Penny Proud

Ty Underwood

Yazmine Vash Payne

Maya Shawatza

not to mention those who die

livin' in the open-air prisons

of our

internal-inhumanities

privileges

unleashed.

Will you have time in the morning,

to stop killing

those who don't

have a calvary

or whiteness

on fleek?

If not,

could you please

at the least

repurpose your sword?

This Ain't Shade Baby, It's Just Tea With No Cream:

Surrender,
Brown Refuge &
Black Homes

I had suffered so long

wrestled

with the fear of you

dark boy

finding me in my dreams and

doing things that I…

The fear of you

would cause me to sweat

leak

peak

but it would be sacrilege to speak of the throbbing secrets that

existed between my mind and the heat drenched

pillows that counseled me to escape from home,

from the grasps of

Blue-back men

finding me in my hiding space.

It terrified me

to know that they

knew me in a special way.

Knew the passageway to my inner truths,

knew their tongues spoke for parts of me that had no business being heard

out loud.

God didn't give the thighs a voice,

but apparently, through you

she intended for them to be heard

speaking in tongues.

High-yellow man-childs'

were my refuge of convenience. I wasn't impressed or hypnotized

by any exotic notion

of difference or the countenance of white supremacies

trying to unlearn me of the beauty of the diversity of blackness

and the richness of a deep onyx, cocoa chocolate

oil black and smooth brother. I hid in the bakery of high yellow

mixes for their warmth, their sweet cakes and intrigue for what

i could give them. They wanted all my stuff and I knew they'd never get it.

No (love) life based in fear will ever last.

Blue-Back Man

72

I run no more. I no longer fear the depth of your touch, the truth of your eyes and the risk of disconnection after the locking of lips, hips and ass or the disengagement of departing dicks, kisses and laughter. To know you at all, is to know that the world is here for me to hold, too. To know that my oak-brown flesh is worthy of love and not just a color-coded potpourri of jack'd fucks, fleeting kisses and attempts to be seen as the exceptional BlaQueer..

Perhaps that was the greatest fear of all. To believe that my tea was

strong

and sweat enough,

worthy to be touched

undiluted,

by the cream.

Your Mother Was A Radical

Birthing a black child, in a world committed to black death, is the

revolutionary act of the 21st Century.

Your mother was a radical.

Don't let her down.

Continue the tradition

of carrying-on,

living through,

defying death

and being

you.

You radical particle

freely flowing

from invisibility to

hypervisibility to demand

create and make way

for your livelihood.

A humanity always known, yet

rarely, fairly, articulated in

the news or rooms where opinions are made

truth. Proclaim yourself here,

present

and unbossed. For

your mother was a radical

and you weren't born

to die to yourself.

Thank your mother,

she is all we know

of love

and self

and tomorrow.

This _Is_ For you

Co-written with Amir Dixon

This is to mi hermano on the block selling ass to keep a roof over his head and food in his stomach. Hoping not to get sexually harassed by the cops and locked up for condom possession

This is to my gurls storming the pavements across the globe. From London, to Uganda, Johannesburg to Tokyo, to Dallas, from New York down to Mississippi. Check list: full beat face. CHECK/. Nasty pumps. CHECK/ red lipstick CHECK/ mase and taser CHECK and CHECK!

This is to my brothers working three jobs to make it through grad school, we see you

This is to my brothers slinging rocks to take care of his brothers and sisters, because he feels he has no other choice

This is to the writer whose puts pen to paper to note words that cut, lives that kill and deaths that heal.

This is to that young activist; who dares to be visible for those of us who too often are waged invisible

This is for full lips, thick hips and tight traps…

This is for tatted chests, scarred hearts and whipped backs..

This is for callous hands, hot-heads and sharp tongues..

This is for phenomenal men who..

This is in remembrance of those who taught that we are not the only ones.. This is for my brothers who dare to love other brothers in a revolutionary way

This is for limp wrist warriors, full of sugar, dripping honey and snatching the create energy of the cosmos

This is for the choir boys, ministers, and ushers praying, hoping and calling for Heaven—here and now—who refuses to divide black from queer, queer from male and Him into itty, bitty, homophobic bite-size pieces..

This is for the man-child, always man, sometimes child, because duality is
how we make it to tomorrow

This is for the Survivors, fighting a war within, against cells unrelenting,
brothers not-repenting and community to afraid to love and live in the
presence of H.I.V.

We. See. You.

This is for to the sons bursting from concrete jungles, craving light, pro-
ducing love and brushing gravel from their rose petals.

This is to the boys, father less and groomed into fullness by mothers with
sharp tongues, thick skin and blue-black hearts.

We. See. You.

Standing head and shoulders over the weeds, thickets and storms that
trouble the mind and ache the soul.

We. See. You.

Sons of Apollo. Mahogany skin deep like rivers, strong as mountains but soft and sensual as the cocoa butter that gives lips and hips glisten.

Listen, if you can, to the rhythm of your ancestors. They're calling, watching and holding you. Nat, Malcolm, Thurgood and Assata. Hold On.

Draw upon the power of your onyx traditions. Locs, resistance and precision. Afros, pyramids and songs of nations. Love without bounds, shackles without bonds, freedom, hope and joy unrelenting. Blackness.

This is for you

Truths Unwritten

Laying across my chest like the caress of

lovers long since departed on a cool Sunday

morning, these truths know me

and I them

but we refuse to speak in public.

They comfort me in times of terror

when I am afraid that I may not make it through another

year's hazing, reminding my soul of

what it has endured, that which cannot be spoken

because my tongue refuses to free that which had imprisoned the body and

nearly killed the spirit. the tongue is loyal, it thinks. The heart is not so

sure.

Unsure about the caress, the silence, the re-memory of all that has tran-

spired. Unsure about holding a comforting grimness or the energy it sucks

or the darkness holding blackness captive.

The soul longs for a rupture. A divorce. A cathartic freeing. It holds no

care for the consequences of Truth but only that Truth's presence will in-

vigorate and free, to invigorate and free.

The mind calculates. What is the cost? Can they be noted before they are exponential? Who will be lost and who will be saved? Are we speaking of scars or tattoos? Beauty marks or blackened pores? Is this redemption or re-sentencing? The mind calculates but the answer remains undefined, error..present but illegible.

The Chameleon's Folly

Chameleons are rookies in my presence. They

fumble through their repertoire attempting

to blend or simply exist

in a world that posits them as both

prey and predator.

The R/Evolution Will Take Your Children
Baltimore In Labor

The revolution won't come because a couple respectable folks of color
went to congress.

Sharpton. Jackson. et al.

The revolution won't happen because we held hands, sang and prayed to
be "delivert."

the hegemony of "non-violence" and the ghosts of the 60's

The revolution will not come because a couple of righteously enraged
brothers and sisters lit their own hoods on fire.

cathartic riots

The revolution will not come because we chanted black lives matter, quot-
ed bell hooks or modernized feminisms and critical race theory.

Not just theory, not just practice, not just aspirational slogans..but praxis,
love ethics, imaginative re/Deconstruction

The revolution will not happen because we used the proper channels of protest, non-violently.

the masters tools will never turn against him, they are in/of/for his/her service

The revolution will not happen because we violently seized a few random, cis white folks for breathing while white.

violating white bodies reifies the need for black systemic control, obliteration

The revolution will not happen because some over educated negro pontificated on Facebook..

who the fuck are we/i/you really writing for?

It will be all these things.

Together

It will not be pretty.

but it will hurt

People will die.

by design

Systems will collapse on folks,

on those we live for,

and they will be consumed.

There will be no peace, and blood will be on all of our hands.

Power concedes nothing by choice,

except violence.

Change has almost always been birthed through a violent process.

We must wake up and reckon with it.

Nurture it through infancy to adulthood and sacrifice for it.

Many have died due to our inaction.

Let that never again be the case.

No More Freddie Gray's.

Baltimore is birthing

something

rageful

r/evolutionary.

BEware.

QUOTES
&
AFFIRMATIONS

A Litany for Survival

Dear White People:

Stop shooting up the world!

Signed,

A Concerned Negro

Sex is often like communion. We keep coming by faith
and sometimes, we get caught up in the spirit and
catch a miracle. Other times you wonder when it will it end,
giving the obligatory amen. However, now I channel my
inner Mother Shirley, run the aisle, and tell my neighbor to
hold my mule!

~

Even sex with loved ones can be triggering.
The body remembers, hears and resists familiar
violences, no matter how sweet or sexy the intent.

Daily, we recreate gender and invest in its (often fixed) reality. Perhaps more often than that.

~

I don't believe in Affirmative Action. It posits the lie that black folks and other folks of color are laying in wait for the affirmations of folks long hell-bent and subsisting off of our desolation. No, if anything, what we need is Corrective Action: those policies, ideas and practices that focus on correcting the centuries long mistake of a nation—if not entire continents—dismissing and outlawing the humanity of black and brown folks.

If our lives could be expressed by the word alone, we'd have nothing left to live for.

~

Queerness is more than mere performance. It is the strange commitment to the idea that folks born free should live free, with excellent food, ideas and insurmountable love at their disposal.

The cosmos have an interesting way of working.
Sometimes you are gifted with supreme beauty and serenity
and other times, you are kindly reminded of things you
never intend to experience, see, feel or perhaps
be inclined to imagine. When the latter occurs,
it is simply a call to shake loose, move forward and
breathe in the oxygen of self-love and holistic care.

We do a lot of work to make sense of violence. Crucial to our logic of suffering is our investment in the constructed truth and nature of gender and race.

~

Peace is not the absence of chaos, violence or uncertainty, it a recognition of their integral role in the journey of the living. Peace is the knowing that what can happen, may very well happen, and that is ok. It is knowing that pain is not the end, but simply a recognition that something else, something un-discovered, is bubbling toward the surface and calling our attention. Peace is the calling of uncertainty, clashes, hopes, plans and redemption to the threshing floor. It is the fleshing out of reality from imaginative re/deconstruction. It is a call to live, allowing our feet, our hearts, our minds, our spirits and our collective selves to always move forward.

The logic of law is best understood as a silent, public marriage of various ideologies understood as and procreating power. The most fundamental of these are white supremacy and anti-blackness, as well as capitalism based in the right to contract and be free from sale. When thinking through violence, the state is therefore best understood as a super parent who wields violence--social, cultural, political, economic, corporeal-publicly accepted and understood as the rule of law. This violence, much like that "discipline" visited upon the bodies of children, results in unspeakable traumas that are accepted as necessary and proper checks on human nature. Humans are naturally bad, or uncivilized or unruly. Traumatized children, in this case American families, traumatized and execute violence in the ways that are reared individually--holding for race, gender, class and sexuality-- by the state. Therefore we must hold the state jointly accountable for particular forms of violence as the super-parent and guarantor of original sin: violence and bad (read: trauma-intensive) rearing. When a black woman is convicted for beating her kids—kids the state has deemed as property accessible to legal violence masked as discipline—it must be seen through a theory of transference of trauma and violence mandated through the state's regulation production of violence. We are led to believe that love is pain and this monopoly is best performed by the state.

From the front, we are assaulted by white supremacy,
from behind heterosexism, our sides must contend with masculine
anxieties and internalized isms from class, dialect and religiosity...but
Queer Men of Color must, and do, continue to love. Though dating is a
soul-fuck.

~

Our bodies are worth loving, freely, fiercely and unabashedly. Do not let
the media, nor the fear harbored by the unloved and unlearned fool you.
Being black/brown/mestiza/yellow/mahogany/colored is no precondition,
being queer is no molecular malfunction and being poz or HIV positive is
no sign of leprosy. Every contour of our existences--the compounded tex-
tures of our realities and the flavorful dances of our spirits--are important,
no, necessary, to the alchemy of the universe. We are the salt of the land. If
we shall lose our flavor, what then is the fate of the rhythm of the world?
Whose spiritual force will the earth quake to? Whose vibe will awaken
dormant mountains, waiting to re-fertilize the land? Therefore do not sur-
vive, but strive to thrive and make peace with your complexities.

To ask the BlaQueer of freedom is to conjure a violent experience that paralyzes the tongue and enrages and engages the soul.

~

Sexual attraction is the most honest form of politics but the practice of love is the greatest test of values.

~

Heteropatriarchy obscures the lens of men so deeply that we often cannot note the reality of sexual violence(s), even when they occur on, within and through our own bodies.

Much of what we call a "war on drugs" is a war on those dealing with systemic oppression, utilizing "drugs" to escape the violence of reality. The drug operates as a psychosocial painkiller yet state demolition focuses on the methods of discomfort management--not the production, producers or benefactors of trauma, tragedy and sociopolitical turbulence. Perhaps, we need a war on Economic Violence, Political Violence, Physical Violence, Legal Violence & SocioCultural Violence...but who would fight and fund the war?

~

Love, at its core is both ethos and practice. It is a self practice, a relationship practice and a communal practice that is real and aspirational. It is a political declaration and orientation. When we say "I love you" not only are we speaking about myriad affections and a commitment to have ones back, but also a promise to nurture ones soul and putting your interests in conversation, in equilibrium with my own.

In many ways modern queer politics and feminisms are neoliberal capitalisms dipped in marginalized dialectics. While there is certainly nothing wrong with wanting to be treated like a human being--pay equity, marriage equality, gender equality and tax issues--there is something wrong our notion of humanity is based off the archetypical white, social mobile, (upper) middle-class male. In many cases, we have started to demand is equal access to cisheteropatriarchy, equal access to the fruits and blood of capitalisms, equal access to imperialism. Queer & Feminists politics cannot be about becoming (hu)man. They must be about redefining what humanity is, providing alternative for what we could be and creating roadmaps to freedom patriarchy, capitalisms, state and racial-sexual terrorisms. I have no problem with equality, but do not call it justice. Call it by its name: access.

~

I looked upon it like the sun, in the midst of relentless winters--only to find that it, capitalism, was a desert, the scion of death valley, beckoning the living to die in a mirage of meritorious renewal.

My adulthood has been equally split from recovering from the physical violence of men and the emotional and verbal violence of women, carried over from my childhood brain. I had to realize, I was still asking permission to be me and pleading for mercy from oncoming blows; asking for a power only I could grant. Love the children around you, not simply by word and provision, but by loving words and exposure to loving acts of kindness in the midst of whatever hells you must endure together.

~

They want to bury our children. We cannot let their memories be eaten by the moth nor the maggot. We must resurrect them, daily. We must show the wreckage of the "just" society we live in. We must live and carry on, as always, but it is not our duty to do so peacefully; carrying internal, eternal violence while behaving. We must erupt, destroy and rebuild. Only then can we bury our dead. Only then can we give honor and tribute for their battles to the end.

The saddest part about today isn't that we are burying another black child. The saddest part about today is that burying a black child killed by police is normal and not a moment conjuring a national soul-check. Tamir Rice was lynched and everybody knows, ever black body felt it and every white body dealt it.

PROSE
Flesh, Bones, & Intellect

Cheers To The Children: Memories of Poverty, Mother/Brother/Otherhood & Blackness

"It was another one of those nights," I thought to myself as I held my younger brother and sisters in my arms. The lights had once again gone out, and it was by no means an accident, the first time or a shock. It was simply a reminder of the lives that we had somehow been born into. I caressed their arms and played with their hair as I sang "This Little Light of Mine." That was back when I still had some semblance of faith. I believed that, if nothing else, the blood of Jesus would surely save us from the darkness of this Section 8 House or the depth of the emptiness within our growing hearts. I knew Jesus would save us from this parasitical life we had been given. Surely it was a trial. Surely we destined for greatness. For God knew the plans he had for us...that is when I had faith, or rather, faith had me.

Thinking quickly, I reminded my siblings that I was the undisputed champion of hide and go seek. I reminded them that this was a prime opportunity for them to prove that they could beat me, lest I remain the greatest and they would have to do as I said until the next game, at an undetermined time. This was an old go-to for me. The house was more mysterious than scary and more fortress of hope and imagination than the marker of poverty, instability and blackness in the dark than when the lights of reality sat upon us. We played hide and seek for hours, until we found she came home. It must have been one of those nights. She needed a fix. Perhaps one of her special friends was afoot. Perhaps she was doing what she had to do to get the lights back on, she did that often. Those were things that were never to be spoken out loud. They were expensive. They cost her things–things I didn't know how to say but could mark and note. That's why I respected her even when heart-ached. She was doing the best she could. She was mortgaging her health, safety and value of her body so that we might eat, sleep and enjoy electricity and heat. W e were feeding off her body. Her mind wasn't always there. This work requires consistent numbing: anxiety medications, deep depression, muscle relaxers. There is no escaping violence that enters your flesh. You cannot wash it off. Not even when your work is done and kids are grown..it resides in you, despite your admonishments for it to leave. Her mind, body and soul have been marked with our names and their blows. She was being a mother, we were being too children. I was being a father-brother, a man-child, knowing and feeling, working and growing, but never fast enough to protect her from the violence of survival necessary to keep us afloat, together, full and growing. She produced love from her sacrifices and daily decisions to live another day. She demonstrated an unconditional love, imperfect in prac-tice, but unrivaled in passion, depth and superhuman abilities. I carry her in my spirit, and continue to build, perfect and struggle with her practice of love.

She wasn't home often but she was always present, even when high, drunk or gone for weeks. I carried her in my heart. She resided in the way I combed and twisted my sister's hair before school, as a strong tenderness and a physical investment of what we might become and bulwark against what society and other folks might portray us as: poor, black,ugly and stuck. She existed in the hugs and kisses I gave my brother, and even the roughest of my friends, a loving tenderness undeterred by the rejection, surprise or maltreatment of its intended recipients. They needed love, but just did not know how to receive it without disarming themselves in a war against perceived victimization and preying. Black boys and girls have to be strong, lest we be devoured whole, in the streets. Bites are constantly taken out of our flesh and psyche. We were consumed for the amusement of bystanders who wished to touch "nappy" hair, ebony flesh and negro culture. Our struggles were positioned as savory morsels in their mouths, only to be chewed, drenched in saliva and regurgitated as mushy perversions of our true essence. They saw us as holes in humanity, we knew ourselves to be the most wholehearted of the living.

He was never present, even when he was there. The heat of Boston's worst blizzard was more impactful than his visits.

Still we carried on. We had no choice. We had to survive, and prayerfully, one day, live and thrive. We were the children of a carry-on tradition, the daughters and sons of despair and diaspora. Our blood has known rivers deeper than the Euphrates and longer than the Nile, carrying intergenerational truths, traumas and practices of survival. If you look closely, deep into our eyes, you might glimpse the source of power, the cosmic connection that tethers us to the divine and roots our bodies in an inextinguishable hope. Anyone who knows both poverty and blackness knows there is nothing more beautiful, strong or resilient than the souls of poor black folk, entombed in strength, courage, wisdom and war.

Anyone who knows both poverty and blackness also knows that there is no escaping either. No matter how far you run, no matter how much money you make, a pound of your flesh and a slice of your soul will remain captive to a war of survivance, long since departed. We cannot forget the taste of hunger on our tongues, no matter how far we've gone from entrees of Miracle Whip and white bread. Cheers to the children who can never forget the art and times of survival jujitsu.

Loving Black Men From Within: A Journey Unsettled.

"They don't know

we need each other

critically.

They expect us to call in sick,

watch television all night

die by our own hands.

They don't know

we are becoming powerful.

Everytime we kiss,

we confirm the new world coming."

Essex Hemphill, American Wedding

Men, especially black men, are taught to hate and fear each other. We are taught that our existence is dependent on our ability to discredit, disavow and destroy those who are similarly situated; in efforts to stand apart from the whole, to stand out as *that nigga*. Our blackness is defined not by its own perfect imperfections, but instead by what their blackness is not, and vice versa. I am strong, because he is a punk. He is a punk, because I am strong. He is not black–or black enough–because I am, therefore his blackness is inadequate, inauthentic and unreal. Alternatively, he is too black, too queer, too other and if I'm situated too close, associated too intimately with him, than I too lose access to the Throne of Normalcy. This is the dance of racial-sexual power, heteropatriarchal musical chairs, the black masculinist Game of Thrones; a silent battle-royale for citizenship. Those who win, die to themselves. Those who lose, win their freedom to subsist alone.

To be exalted and celebrated on the throne of black maleness is the dream of many young black and other male-situated people of color. The sociocultural benefits are endless, if not necessary for survival. Such a champion is seen as virile studs–reminiscent our plantation days–sexually desirable and able to perform Mandingo-esque, orgasmic experiences: individual and communal consent to fuck (men, women, mores) is a birthright. They are strong, immune to emotional violence, and therefore perfectly situated to benefit (read: sideline) women as the heads of household, church and community. The existence of womyn and the autonomy of women is an existential threat to the man whose prestige is predicated on the woman's need for his brash, violent, irreverent, dic(k)tatorial orientation. Their power is proven time and time again on the bodies of lesser champions, pussies and women who dare exhibit notions of independence. Domestic violence, sexual assault, rape, fights and assaultive speech are simply annoying and natural byproducts of the masculine elixir integral to the ongoing circumcision of a real black man.

No tears.

No reflection.

No hugs.

Their words are few.

They are not expected or allowed to think critically, but instead, implored to act swiftly. *You think long, you think wrong.* All judgements are final. This is the decree of society. The fulfillment of this decree results in pop-culture capital and sociopolitical, legal and physical capital punishment: the conundrum of corporeal capitalisms. Violation of such decrees necessitates sociocultural lashing, BlaQueer-bashing, "hip hop-culture" cache and permissive sociopolitical, legal and physical torment.

To exist outside the controlling images, stigmas and stereotypes of black male-hood is the fear black boys confront from a young age, and black women fight from birth. Many have no "choice" but to conform and submit to cultural circumcision. The price of rebellion is real and steep. A child or young adult may face bullying, rape, loss of community, family abandonment and/or a lack of love/affection. No one can make it alone for long, and for a child this is not a choice, it is an issue of survival. However some, by nature or circumstance, exist subtly or loudly outside the bounds of mandated "black" maleness. The ways to do so are myriad, one can be:

108

queer, trans*, humanistic, pacifist, loving, bisexual, feminist, educated, overtly empathetic and/or "articulate." However, this list is not exhaustive and none of these traits are a panacea for the colds resulting from the wily seasons of white supremacy and cisheteropatriarchy.

The outsider is often held up as a threat to the normative, imputed, raced, stereotypical and stigmatized image of the black male. As such, the transgressor is often interpreted as a threat to the health, strength and identity of the whole, as opposed to an integral part of the body. Many see those pushed outside the imputed bounds of blackness as living insults, who see themselves as "better than," "uppity" or "acting white." This robs the "othered" of citizenship or access to home, history, culture, love(s) and community. It also reinforces the false image of black men as a potpourri of animalistic, lethal characteristics: needing, wanting and birthed to be controlled, subdued, owned, operated and eliminated by the police state. Violence against others is used to exalt and illustrate anti-black, extrajudicial and judicial genocides as just, necessary acts of protection for the good of humanity, especially "good black folks." This in turn fuels the animosity between othered black men and stigmatized, "real" black men. This is happening with folks knowing, but not noting, that all black men are both othered and stigmatized at the same time, within the same body, by the same systems, ideologies, peoples and institutions.

The divisions among black men are not only mandated and expected but held up as normal and just. Though we are often seen as a monolith, our differences are selectively held up as a reason to use violence and to denigrate one (or many) at the (marginal) benefit of others. Therefore, it is no surprise, that between us–black men of varying experiences–there often exists a deep reservoir of distrust that few of us dare cross. For years I lived in fear and stewed in a manufactured contempt of blackness to survive, because even as a child, I knew the truth of the apparent permanence of race and cisheteropatriarchy might extinguish my desire to live.

I harbored a deep distrust of all black men. I feared the outwardly masculine and alpha brothers: I would just as soon die as submit to their will(s). I also feared being found out as not truly, wholly one of their ilk. I feared losing my citizenship: access to my family, access to love and the hope of humanity and redemption. I built a sword of blackness, a shield of masculinities and a walk-in closet queer anxieties. I also distrusted the othered, that shit looked contagious. I knew I was one of them, but feared their outward marking was impermissibly infectious. I viewed them as snakes who would betray the race at the drop of a red-cent. What love I had, I gave to black women, ignoring, deriding and avoiding black men at all cost–because I knew we had more in common that I could ever handle. My identity is intimately linked with all of them–my brothers–othered and normative. They are me and I am them. It wasn't until I learned to love myself that I began to understand their importance in my ability to survive, thrive and receive love–and perhaps more importantly–myself. This did not come naturally. It is a battle that is both intentional and eternal, internal and external. In re-membering the truths of myself, the truths of us, the constructed lies—and real consequences—of gender, race, sexuality and class; I'm learning to birth an ethic that demonstrates that Black Lives Matter to me, because of me and despite me. To recall that truth, is to embrace our diversity and know that our fleshy differences are largely immaterial to cosmic kinship.

Why Black Men Loving Black Men Is A Revolutionary, Suicidal Act

"Black Men Loving Black Men

Is the Revolutionary Act

of the 1980s"

-Joseph Beam

The first time I happened upon that quotation by the great Joseph Beam, it did a work on my spirit. I was just shy of 16 and almost delivered from the Church of God in Christ (COGIC), yet still an occasional, holy rollin' backslider; the oil was too strong. To my young soul, it illuminated the possibility of a self and communal love that didn't lead to the burning or gnashing of flesh, but instead to a fire that melted oppression, causing black men to spring forth clean and powerful as onyx Phoenix. Just shy of 16, I was already grown, but Joey B gave me a new lease on life, I moving from closeted to confident. That was 2005. It is now 2015.

In the decades since, something in me has changed. I won't say I'm grown, quite yet, but I have grown into a deeper understanding of self, sex and the practice of love. I have come to understand that to revolt, or to inspire revolution, means to act, live, love, think, fuck and die in opposition to an entrenched system while midwifing one of a liberatory nature–

112

with the power to undo all that you think you are–all remaining true and whole to self, eschewing the notion of an "other." Revolution will undo you. If it does not, you have not yet revolted within or, put simply, unbecome what hegemonic, white supremacist, capitalistic, cisheteropatriarchal society has branded upon your flesh and psyche. The iron is hot and it's markings are not easily removed. Therefore, internal revolution is nothing short of psychosocial laser removal treatment–from thought to flesh. For black men, this requires a role-reversal and an expertise in survival jujitsu and imaginative reconstruction.

Black Men Loving Black Men…

This quotation is recited at every black gay/sgl/bi/dl/_____ con-ference and is generally followed by snaps, smiles and a high/low chorus of YASSSSSS! But what is often heard, understood and practiced is fuck-ing, not loving, or even lusting. If we look closely we can understand the complex relationship between black men as a collective practice of fuck-ing; a rough, quick, thorough, sweaty and primal intercourse that offers short-term relief for a long term desire, repeated over time, in almost any space we enter. The relationship between our sociopolitical bodies, our *selves*, brother-to-brother becomes a practice of orientation. More often than not, we measure our masculinities, wealth, worth, humanity and de-sirability in opposition to those around us. We do so, acting as if the beau-ty and bounds of blackness are limited, and our preferred place in the imaginary white supremacist spectrum of blackened humanities can only be secured by the expulsion or demotion of another black brother. The thinking then goes, that there can only be so many "good" and "worthy" or "real" black men. To think otherwise strikes at intermingled notions of the children of capitalism–the exceptional negro/talented tenth mythology (ex: Barack/Oprah)–and white supremacy–the inherent/imputed deficiency of blackness (ex: controlling images: laziness, violence, hyper-sexuality).

Anti-Blackness is a convenient, socially constructed covering of white supremacy, white anxiety and white violence.

Black men, like all men, are given situational power and privilege in relation to women of their racial location. It must be clearly noted that black men–across space, time, class and sexuality–have used this privilege and access to power, to both uplift and more often than not, decimate black women. This has been completed and articulated by the masses as black men accessing and appropriating (white) patriarchy. This is true. However, I posit that it is directly linked to the concept of racial inferiority–a child of white supremacy, a sibling of anti-blackness–that implicitly notes that in order for black men to access whiteness "humanity," we must first differentiate ourselves from other black people (read: women, womyn, queers, trans* folk). Differentiating and othering in the United States is marked by power and power is understood through the demonstration of a marked inability to be oppressed and owned; while simultaneously, ruthlessly portraying that power, through the ability, desire and provision of oppression, ownership and propertying of the othered. Through this violent quest for power, and perhaps the illusion of freedom, black men as a group are marked as violent, hyper-sexual, immoral, criminal and in need of state-control/lashing. The prophecy, markings, and controlling images of white supremacy and anti-blackness become proven by the actions of black men, performing these lip synced lyrics and scripts from the master's tongue.

Violence upon, and violations of/through, the black male body are the pre-ferred redemptive practice of 21st century.

Aside from black women, black men are the primary target of black male patriarchy and power-lust. Sexism is well embedded in society, therefore, the greatest actual threat to a black man's access to (white supremacist) power in the black community is another black man. This conversation and theory is well fleshed out in bell hook's "We Be Real Cool" and Richard Majors and Janet Mancini Billson's "Cool Pose : The Dilemmas of Black Manhood in America." Both speak to the ways in which black men across age protect themselves–through violence, silence and other performances–against the indignities of white supremacy, anti-blackness, poverty, masculine anxiety and discrimination in their communities. We are taught to prove our worth through the devaluation and violation of other black men. In these practices of violence, distancing and differentiation we are positioned as distinct, if not circumcised, from the collective "bad" black body. We are the strong, the smart, the responsible, the tolerant, the feminist, the queer, the anti-racist, the well-read, the masculine, the Christian; the last buffer against the highly contagious other. We are given purpose, we are given worth and we are given pseudo-whiteness, through our performance, perfection and articulation of anti-blackness and internalized white supremacies. To do otherwise–articulating or demonstrating a "soft" pose, or denunciation of this parasitic cycle–can leave a

116

brother isolated, ostracized, bloodied and/or dead.

...Is The Revolutionary..

Flipping the script is both revolutionary and radical. It is a revolt against all that has been designated as "blackness" and radical–or grasping at the root–of the tenants of white supremacy and anti-blackness. Transgressing this ideology and ethic, with a practice of love is not only unheard of, but an unnatural practice in a white supremacist state. This is certainly true if we begin to use my dynamic conception of a critical love ethic: "a practice of universal liberation from cyclical and systemic violence and oppression...we must look deeply and examine the oppressor within, dare to love those who we see as threats or "other" and question whether the threat is real, imagined or internal. This is a call for a human solidarity across and beyond racialized differences and an ethic of love that first acknowledges our shared humanity and endeavors to reify that shared notion." As I stated in earlier piece on love among black men, we must begin to reconstruct our notions of self, our relationship to others, brothers and sisters.

> *"The reactionary suicide is 'wise,' and the revolutionary suicide is a 'fool,' a fool for the revolution in the way Paul meant when he spoke of being a 'fool for Christ,' That foolishness can move mountains of oppression; it is our great leap and our commitment to the dead and the unborn."*

– Huey P. Newton, I Am We, or Revolutionary Suicide

We must engage in communal euthanasia of blackness as we've accepted
it and come to practice and believe that:

The tea is, blackness is the essence of creation, a potpourri of the creative ingredients of existence. Blackness, unbought, unbossed and unrestrained is the building block of color and from its presence, our presence, your presence, derives all things. …

From "A Love Letter To My Black Gay Brothers"

Our ancestors have done their work; gifting us with a bloody and loving legacy of overcoming and carrying-on, together. It is now our duty to continue to expand these notions of "love," "Blackness" and "togetherness."

The Raping(s), The Reaping, The Humanistic Renewal

No solutions are presented here, just memories of lives lost and survived.
Triggers: Rape, Molestation, Religion, Domestic Violence, Suicide, Apathy

"Living in a world they didn't make...

Living in a world that's filled with hate...

Living in a world where grown-ups break the rules"

Janet Jackson, Livin' In A World (They Didn't Make), Rhythm Nation 1814

The First Time: A Family Affair

I can't feel the first time, but my body will never forget the second, third, fourth and fifth times. Perhaps I was too young. Perhaps my three, five or seven-year old self had no distinct understandings of sex or sexuality, especially not molestation or rape. I remember not remembering. I had been separated from my *self*. I knew that something was wrong. I remember him sliding into the bed every night after grandma went to sleep. I remember the rocking of the bed. I remember his hot breath on my ear and his toothy promise that "I'm going to rock your world." Then I stopped remembering, for years.

The truth is, I wanted him to rock my world. My world was in disarray. Rocks don't move until they are acted upon by the universe or some great outside force. I was always moving. Moving between mom and dad, maternal and paternal grandmothers, stability and turbulence, stable turbulence. I was a homeless, motherless child but I cannot say I was loveless. My grandmothers made sure of that, and so did he. He who must not be named. I wanted his love—not sexually. I hadn't awoken to queerness then. But I wanted him to be my brother, no, my father, no…I wanted to be him. He wasn't just cool, he was that dude. He was the fastest runner in the state and an even better basketball player, and let's not get started on football. I wanted to run like that. I wanted everyone to cheer. I wanted to be seen.

I was never heard. No matter how many spelling bees I learned or how many large, foreign words I memorized—perfectly mind you—I was never heard. Except by him, he had always heard me and smiled. He looked into my eyes when I spoke of the silliest things that young boys speak of. He was a teenager, barely. No one heard or saw him either, well, no one he loved. He gave me an identity, but he took something too.

After I forgot to remember, I lost all my dreams. He stole them. My creative, beautiful, life-saving dreams. They were my hiding place. I remember now. I remember how I'd fall asleep to the bloody screams of my mother, as my sisters' father would terrorize and beat her within half-gasps of death, only to awaken with an awkward smile on my face because in my dreams I ruled supreme. My mind had transformed my mother's terror and pain into a locust of her power. I'd dream my mother had mind control like the Phoenix in X-Men and would make our "father" hang himself by the nook of his shirt, while beating the blood from his face with those huge, terrible hands. She never killed him. My mother was too sweet for that. I had often prayed that she would though. She was too strong for murder. A strength I later found within myself. I dreamt of good things too, but I can't remember. My dreams and memory were stolen, aside from violence, hot breath, night-time whispers and bloody screams for death.

He wanted to be seen. He wanted to be seen as a black man. He took a black boy to prove, perhaps, that he was no longer a boy and could no longer be taken. He was a man. It later came out that he was raped too, early and often. Now he's in prison and I'm in law school. Black men eating black boys, being black boys eating black kids: the cycle must end.

Subplot: The UnHoly Trigger

At 15, I was training to be a minister under my pastor. All was going well. I was happy-ish. I had found a new home within the black supremacist, heteropatriarchal, capitalistic, homoantagontistic Church. The parts of me that had been dying as a child were fed and portions of me that had been free in my dreams was chopped liver. I learned to be a happy cannibal. After all, it was God's will. Until it wasn't. That year, at the AIMS conference, the pastor introduced me to a promising minister of music, 15 years my senior. We exchanged numbers. He proceeded to send me countless pictures of his ass, his dick with the phrase "you want to rock my world?"

Then I remembered. Everything at once. It was like I was being burned alive and drowned at the same time. I was hot and could not breathe. I remembered him entering me, first at 7, then at 5, and for the last time at 12. I cried. I shouted. I could feel him. I could feel me, my body, flesh tearing. My heart tore, too. My imagination retired, because it was no match for reality. I had stopped dreaming. He had raped me. Stolen the faculty of my mind. That was when I stopped writing. I didn't trust my mind to roam free anymore. Clearly, it was my fault. I dreamed too much and now my nightmares would consume me. So I stopped dreaming. I stopped remembering. I embraced the death of a part of me.

A friend found me emerging from the floor of my hotel room. He was young and innocent and concerned. I told him I was simply stretching. He said we needed to prepare for revival. In all truths, I had had a revival of my own, right then and there. The minister approached me in the bathroom, later that evening, as I was using the urinal. I grabbed his hard dick and balls as hard as I could, and proceeded to try to pop them off. It didn't work, but I felt better. Felt like I had a handle on things. If nothing else, I knew that a dick wasn't much longer or thicker than my hand and I need not fear any, not even my own, anymore. I left the Church after we returned home and that was that.

The thorn in his flesh was something he could longer bear. He needed to remove it. The myth of Christian perfection, absolution and the wrath of a white, homophobic God nearly killed him. He wanted to release. He wanted to release on me, in me, through me. I am no threshing floor.

The Second Time: Accidental Assassin

We had been friends, the closest of friends. I had recently hit my stride. Life had been hard–my mother was suffering from the side-effects of our "father" coping with sex, love and drugs, lots of drugs–I was still working full-time and doing a share of the love-labor raising my three younger siblings. However, I was happy. Not a day passed when I wasn't smiling. I had started accepting my sexuality. I was dating. I established a strong brotherhood with other gay christian brothers like Randy, Kenneth, Angelo, Jason and Justin. They had healed me. I was whole-ish. We were something; a national brotherhood of the BlaQueers, demanding God's love. Demanding respect from friend, foe and self. Demanding we love each other, and ourselves, without repentance. My archangels. I had recently been accepted to a prestigious school, created by one of my idols. Life was good. I was happy.

He was my best friend. Certainly my closest "straight" friend. I was out by then. Out and free. Out, free and in love with a fiery little, pinoy-boy from Texas. Then it happened. But I suppose I knew it would. My boyfriend warned me to watch out. So did his girlfriend, my good friend–at the time. I wanted to trust. I needed to trust. Trust was new to me. I hadn't known her. I wanted Trust with me all the time. I was naive.

We were celebrating his birthday. He was sipping syrup again. The rest of us were drinking on the mountain top. No one above age. Each of us 17/18ish. Pissed. Falling over each other. We stumbled down the small mountain, pissing on random walls and dodging the campus security. We were having fun. I couldn't remember my name or feel my cheeks. I had tried to throw up, but my stomach was stingy with its contents. Our friends got us to the bathroom. He threw up. They put us in our secret bachelor pad. The first time I woke up, my jeans were unzipped. I was confused and afraid. He was my friend. I must have forgotten to zip them. Strange, they were skinny jeans. They don't open easily. I was exposed. Clearly. I remember a camera flash, giggles and a slamming door. I couldn't open my eyes. They were too heavy. But then I felt it. The clear feeling of viola-tion. Fingers on my dick, then a wetness. A warm wetness. I struggled to roll away. He held my hips. I closed my eyes tighter. Then the wetness on my lips, a kiss, soft at first and then violently aggressive. The loud, raspy whispers of "I'm not a fag." Then, another gentle kiss. No, I kept saying. No. I don't like you. You have a girlfriend. Another kiss. He entered my mouth, and I saw my cousin. I was 7 again and I passed out. I woke up and I ran, shoe-less. First to the top of the mountain, where I cried and cried and cried. I stripped myself naked. I couldn't bear the smell of his must on my clothes. I rubbed my lips until they bled. I didn't want to taste him. I cried some more. Then, for the first time in three years, I prayed, and slept under the darkness.

He had taken my mouth, and with it many friendships and years of survival. I was the gay one, so everyone believed I was the aggressor. I must've wanted it. I clearly wanted it. All gay men want straight guys. All black people want white folks. That was the line. That was supposedly the story he told. The one where some hyper-sexual, predatory, smooth talking black, gay pervert took advantage of him in his sleep. Because I was poor, I was disturbed and clearly wanted something he had. Never mind that I had never had sex of my own volition. Never mind that his girlfriend was my best friend. Never mind that my boyfriend of nine months, often wondered aloud why I hadn't experienced more, sexually, even with him.

For two months, I had one hour of open-air imprisonment. For twenty-three hours, for 58 days, I pondered the ironies of my circumstances. For one hour per day, per week, for eight weeks, I taught the marked among us to read and write and retrace their journey to home, freedom and internal redemption. Years later it came, an email, containing an apology of sorts. It was garbled, but seem to point to state of confusion, a "grey area," he said. I was too startled by the scripture and the reentering of theology into my headspace to be fully consider his words. I wanted to be upset. To be angry. I want to destroy something. Instead, I just wanted to destroy myself. I was numb. So much had been stolen, chiefly Trust. And then, some strange shit happened. I cried for him. I was 22 by then. I showed the email to my boyfriend and he marveled at my ability to continue living and my absence of anger. I marveled at the recognition that I was still alive.

The fuckery. He took my body to feel at home in his own. Tried to take my name to protect his own. Then he wanted my sympathy to redeem himself. There was nothing grey, all I saw was whiteness. White guilt on fleek.

The Third Time: The Power of Blood

We dated for two weeks. Not really dated. We had sex and argued. He hated that I was pledging a fraternity and I hated that he wasn't my ex-boyfriend. He was cute, well-built, with a large head and an even larger smile. The sex was fantastic. For two weeks, we had a great deal of fun and then things started getting quite crazy. I broke it off with him on day 10. He'd show up in my room unannounced and raise all type of hell about my whereabouts, whether I had drunk anything that night, if I still loved my ex, why I didn't want to be with him anymore and then threaten to kill himself if I didn't stay and talk to him. The first few topics I ignored with skill and zeal. The last comment got me every time. He knew that. I had told him of how one of my best friends of suicide, the two other close childhood friends had tried it routinely and I only bailed because I was too chicken shit of the hell Pastor preached of each week. The night before he took what was mine, we argued again and he promised that if we didn't speak he would drive his car off the highway into the river. I agreed to come into his car and talk, where he attempted to kiss me and perform oral sex. I rebuffed him. He began to cry. He then locked the doors and began to drive, fast. Too fast for the potholes of Boston. Swerving here and there, promising to kill us both if we couldn't be together. I was scared as hell, but part of me was hoping he'd do it. Just so I could be done with him and every other deranged man I'd allowed too close to me. We didn't crash or die, but I quickly alerted all of my friends to avoid him at all costs and to

129

refrain from inviting him to any of our spaces. It sounds childish, but he had lost his damn mind.

It never occurred to me to file a police report or make a report with campus police. The last time I talked to police they nearly ended my life and my sanity. No way was I talking to the police about an issue even remotely related to sex or gayness. Not as long as I was black and gay, or whenever I was speaking about a crazy white man. I wish I had spoken to someone, besides my friends. We didn't entertain the thought that this was anything more than just another crazy college story. Until it was too late. A day later, I had gone out drinking with my older fraternity brothers and I was obscenely intoxicated. He called again, threatening suicide. I hung up immediately. When we finally walked through campus, we passed his place and he was sitting the porch crying, begging for help. I walked over and told my brothers it was ok. We cooked some ramen. His roommate, a friend of mine, was out. He wanted me to hold him. I refused. He asked me to tuck him in and stay until he fell asleep. I watched him lay down for as long as I could, before I fell asleep on my friend Carlos' bed. I awoke in pain, searing pain, on my chest, neck, dick and ass. I thought I had caught something. In truth, I had caught something I could never lose, but that wasn't what was burning me up. I quickly got dressed and ran to my room only to be greeted by my best friend and his eyes told me everything. I ran to the mirror and screamed. My body was wrecked. I was covered in black and red bite marks. My ass was still wet with traces of blood. My dick had been rubbed raw. My phone buzzed with a text. "No means yes. Yes means yes. Frat rule, right? Last night was great -P". I cried more. Logan held me, as I cried and cried and finally, after about an hour the tears released me. Then I realized what he had wanted all along. Power. He wanted my power. I cried, and I smirked. I needed to go for a walk. I would not be used. I went to the old slave quarters and called upon the ancestors for strength and awareness and wisdom. I called for love. I called for forgiveness. I called for understanding. I called for me. I called out their names: Belinda, Celia, Frederick…mothers, fathers and others who had endured more violent scenes than I, for help. I called their names too: S, T, P. I had never stopped carrying them in my body, on my mind, like sexual brandings still searing my essence.

Dominating, controlling and violating me gave him power and a freedom he could not afford without my flesh. He needed to survive. This black flesh. This black, scarred flesh fueled and cooled his anxiety ridden existence of being too femme, too gay and not quite white enough. His father told him he was no man. He was proving that here and now, as he bit, spit and violated me.

The Healing(s)

Healings are an ongoing practice, but they began with the practice and promise of absolute self-love. I began each day by looking in the mirror and reminding myself that I was alive, that I deserved to be alive, that I was loved and that I worthy of love. I promised myself, daily, in the mirror, that I would not be killed by the sickness of others, by my circumstances or my station in life or despair. I promised to use my pain for power and progress. I promised to remember and not forget. I worked on my hate, especially my self-hate. I began to Trust my gut. I read bell hooks, religiously, to ascertain what a love practice might look like for me. I began to tell it all. All my truths. All my traumas. All my fears. All my fuck-ups to anyone who dare be a friend, a lover, or family. Some rejected me. Some stood/stand in cold silence, perhaps in guilt or disbelief. Many wonder how this could happen to one person, and if so, why I would let it happen, what *had I* done to be in such precarious situations? Others ask why I responded how I did. I don't have answers for them. I won't try to think of answers. I answer to myself and the Universe.

In many ways, I've become able to understand what I've experienced as an important part of my existence. I now have a deep sensitivity for people; their interpretations of events, the volatility of emotions and the desire and fear of (dis)connection. I understand now, that the fucking of my body and raping of my essence was more than the result of a few deranged, pained boys and men. More than anything, what I survived, was about the unresolved violences of peoples suffering in silence, a silence created by dutiful acquiescence to systems of systemic, external and internal domination. My life has been forever changed with each rape or sexual assault, but by the grace of the Cosmos, I've been able to take back who I was and become more of who I am destined to be. I made the pivotal decision to choose to love humans or hate them–including myself. Humans unrestrained, untaught and unloved are tomorrow's monsters. I recognize and believe that my propensity to be free or monstrous, is directly tied up with that of all who breathe. It is therefore my duty to produce and cultivate a radical love and investment with/for/through humanity in all it's fuckery. Not everyone has had this opportunity. Not everyone survives. Some are killed, physically and/or psychologically. As someone gifted with thebreathe of life, I feel a personal duty to help midwife a world where such violences are killed at conception.

Sexual violence, like all personal violations, are heinous acts. But they must be confronted head on and dealt with. We are dealing with more than depraved hearts and minds. We are dealing with a peoples who have lost or auctioned off their humanity. As rape and sexual assault become less invisible on campuses across the nation, scholars, advocates and fellow survivors have begun to call out, name and castigate a violent "rape culture." I too, have seen and experienced a performance of gender and power and self—in my fraternity, on my campus, in my friends, family and in myself—but this is not simply about culture or miseducation. I have come to believe that "rape culture" is a misleading short hand for an analysis of something fundamentally constitutive of western society. Rape is not a culture, otherwise we, as a people would've adjusted accordingly, swiftly. Cultural shifts simply require the changing of hearts and minds, often through a moment(s) of great tragedy and/or awakening: the amount of rape and sexual assault on black men and womyn through slavery and Amerikkka's existence has not provided that jilt. This is not about culture. Rape is something else, perhaps a tool, a tool for power accumulation and dehumanization, a tool that is gendered--yes, I mean gender not sex--raced and classed. The constitutive parts of western society come together in the act/tool/violence of rape to transform the violated human into a sort of property, a bag flesh that is to be used as pleased—to broken to resist—but particularly to produce pleasure, power and ultimate visibility and valida- tion of these aforementioned sociopolitical al goods. Rape then, is a sort of base distillation of corporeal capitalisms, often mystified by its racial, gendered, classed, sexual and political components. To be raped is not simply to be fucked or sexually violated, but to instead be politically dis- membered and chattelized in your own flesh; where only the state can avenge you, as a ward/owner of sorts, leasing you to provide the ultimate argument for ongoing, ultimate state control of other bodies not unlike (y)our own. This shit is systemic. I refused to be raped, owned or ma- ligned by the same system that stole my history. Instead, I choose my hu- manity and alternative forms of justice that don't involve state-violence through or because of my flesh. I remember what it feels like to be raped, far away from home, and to lose my dreams. To those that know this story, forgetfulness will not protect us. We must remember. We must go home. We must change course, or risk losing the few dreams we have left.

Black, Gifted & Privileged: Confronting Intraracial Power In The Age of Trayvon

When a person of color is killed by a police officer, or badgeless vigilante, it exposes and strikes at the moral fabric of America but more viscerally at the psyche of every person of color with a beating heart. Each strike, blow or shot to their flesh pierces through our collective identity in ways sometimes articulated by great poets, demonstrated by activists old and emerging and mapped by social workers, theorists and spiritual gurus. Much more often, however, we do not have words or faculty to articulate the fire that emanates within our bones; gifting us with a source capable of birthing both revolutionary rage and cancerous infernos. There are simply those things cannot be spoken, because the tongue was never meant to fathom such violences.

"A bird doesn't sing because it has an answer. It sings because it has a song."

-Maya Angelou

During the most recent trend of state-sanctioned, or explained, violence on black womyn and men, I've been at three strikingly different institutions (Tufts, Berkeley & Howard Law). Tufts is an elite "little Ivy," a predominantly white institution, just outside of Boston. It is drenched in white-liberal progressive politics, with a tradition hewing close to that of a Unitarian practice, strongly flavored by liberal Jewish culture. The school is lily white with a sprinkling of people of color–many of whom are first generation college students–with a deeply radical core. Howard Law, on the other hand, is a historical black university (HBCU), and has an iconic tradition of moderate to radical black social justice movements. Many of my peers at Howard Law are nestled firmly in the middle class, if not the upper middle class, but a few of us Section 8 types slipped through the cracks. In both cases, the response to the murders of black peoples has been the same. Students organize. We debate. We learn. We cry. We struggle to cope with the privilege of our location and our increasing distance from the realities of everyday black folk. Perhaps the most popular trend has been to link our livelihoods to those of the slain and surviving with T-Shirts and hoodies stating "I Can't Breathe" or "I Am Trayvon." This is understandable but more akin to identity affinity than power realities.

As a participant and sometimes leader in many of my campuses' movements, I've experienced both heartache and empathy at these responses: feeling both a sense of commonality and hope, as well as a searing sense of guilt, opportunistic therapies and liminality. The fact of the matter is, I can breathe and I am not Trayvon, Renisha, Ezell, or Tamir. I am here. While I face many systemic and sociopolitical challenges, threats violences and obstacles as a BlaQueer male, raised on food-stamps and Section 8, I am still here and moving quite fast from there: that place where my flesh and blood, my mothers, brothers and sisters live. It's un- likely as a JD, and soon to be PhD student, that I will routinely find myself in a situation or geographic location where police will regularly practice stop & frisk. My growing and compounding privileges will continually afford me a layer of protection–albeit quite less than whiteness–that my brothers and sisters, nieces and nephews, might never know. The majority of my time–no matter how much I profess to work with or for the people– will be spent behind lecterns, podiums and teleprompters, no matter how much time I spend in community. I will be hustling and dealing with mi- cro-aggressions, but in boardrooms, coffee shops, faculty meetings and at the very least, behind the albeit thin veneer of my cultural capital. More often than not, I'll be lauded for not being "those people," my people: which of course, is a violence of its own, but it will never kill me.

Graduate and undergraduate school has the power to provide social and economic capital to black and Latinx youth. If we are able to navigate these often white-supremacist, cisheteropatriarchal, capitalistic, nativist spaces–and escape with a fragment of our souls and ethics in tact–there is an elusive promise that we might achieve the success our foremothers and ancestors had long sacrificed for us. However, in many cases, this acquisi- tion of situational privilege–in our quests to gain wealth(s)–often robs us of the richness of home. Within our families we sometimes become pariahs, not because we think we are better, or our family sees us as worse, but because our newfound privilege (and sometimes world-views) are the Onyx elephants at the table. While we experience and note the growth in the physical, social, and political distance from our families–we also become hip to the distance from those in our educational spheres. We understand many academic and sociopolitical questions through the textured lenses from which we've come, a world unfamiliar to many of those who run our schools, as well as the kids we destroyed in beer-pong last weekend. We are foreigners in the land. And, perhaps most salient to this piece, is the fact our authenticity is now challenged on every front. We are simultaneously casts as not black enough (read: too educated), not smart enough (read: too black), too conservative (read: career-minded), radical (read: human-centered) and hypersensitive (read: culturally competent). These markings exist in the minds of those often most consequential in our lives: family, professors, supervisors and "friends" and all too often have the effect of pushing us into a place where we are neither here nor there, neither strangers nor community members, but living battlefields for the political and sociocultural supremacy.

In effect, we often experience our lives as stateless peoples, who exist in a liminal, unnamed social position. We know of our condition, as do the professionals and scholars that came before us, but it remains an open secret. It would be uncouth to speak of the trauma of situational privilege, that thing we kill ourselves for daily, in a communal ritual of cultural euthanasia. Who are we to whine about the stresses of managing multiple consciousnesses that, at times, overwhelm our neuronal pathways to the point of exhaustion: where we forget what role we should be performing in the moment, which inflection to use, when our skin tone is proper for the zone? It seems silly to speak of the school as a spiritual and ideological war-zone when thousands die across the nation from police interactions, gun violence and other symptoms of the war on black and blackened poor peoples. Who are we to speak of pain when poor people are made invisible and swept under the feel good blanket of "middle class" politics? We got out. We are moving on up. We don't quite know where to, but we are told it is a good place. It is distant. Far from *our families*. We mustn't worry about them, this distance is good for our career, we are told. We must be separated to learn to lead, as if the education system has every taught any black person what they didn't already know about surviving the dual plague of white supremacy and capitalism. In all truth, we are being taught and trained to be different; to be professionals. To profess, speak of and bear witness to a life—an ideology—that is not only different than that from whence we came but also superior. We are slowly transformed into ambassadors of American elitism and our black flesh is transformed, as we accumulate wealth and situational prestige, into proof and authentication of the silently violent sociopolitical and legal power structure that we live in. Our success becomes proof that the most, if not all, social ills are not baked into the system or nation but instead a sad indication of a character flaw in the bones of several million people. They could've done better, the logic goes and our bodies prove, if they simply worked harder, worked smarter and gave a damn. Professionalism, with its bowties and pantsuits and relaxers and fresh lineups and learned inflections and branded predilections is a costly performance, a ritual that provides partial absolvement to some and sure death to others; the mothers, fathers and kinfolk of the newly learned.

Many of us are learning to unlearn. Yet here is much that we do not know, chiefly, how to navigate these seemingly oppositional spaces without losing our future, abandoning our pasts or sacrificing our peace. What we do know is, we are in a place that many have lost blood, sweat and tears for, all with hopes that we might one day stand on their shoulders and reach the proverbial mountaintop. We know that we are our mother's sons and daughters, but worlds apart from the conditions of our rearing. Still and yet, there exists a desire to reach back, pull forward, and take care of home. But how do we do that, authentically, without papering over the fragile privileges we now possess? How do we show solidarity with the slain and surviving without being struggle-blind, and refusing to provide for the differences in our present existences and social locations? We know that we may never be Eric Garner, but our nieces and nephews, brothers and sisters, cousins, uncle and aunts, might just be.

Therefore, we must realize that we cannot continue to operate as a "talented tenth" that knows best for our peoples. Instead, we must first note–and admit–the power and privilege that has come from the struggle of luck and opportunity. We must offer our skills, resources and talents as supplements to the strategies of those most impacted, and continue to empower and affirm them as the leaders and experts that they are. This is not to say that we should sit on our laurels, and watch the most burdened carry the heaviest loads, but a reminder that we would do well to listen–sometimes in disagreement–before positioning ourselves as the saviors of our kin. As beneficiaries of a system that is feeds off of our kin, we are called to move past partial patronage and began a process of disinvestment from economic and cultural violence, while investing in and helping to imagine an alternative system of thriving. We all face struggle and discrimination, the intersections of lived realities, opportunities and obstacles. However, our present, compounded existences must be reckoned with, if we are ever to come together as an impenetrable force of liberation, justice and healing. I have always attempted to take "home" with me, wherever I go, but in the years to come, I've learned that home is my not my property but a free companion. I endeavor to let "home" be a co-pilot on our journey, and not just a passenger.

Cosmic Reconciliations & Divine Divestments: BlaQueerness, Masculinities and Community

BlaQueer community members, scholars, artists, lovers and griots have long discussed the effects of normative masculinities on our livelihoods and our struggles with and against the hegemonic portrayal of maleness. While (white) maleness is often defined and recognized as the paragon of human existence–economically, physically, intellectually–black maleness has been imprisoned in controlling images as a type of mutation. Black masculinity is similar to white masculinity insofar that neither tolerate femininities—its existence often depends on ongoing, silent, violations of them—and both are situated in the sociopolitical domination and dominion over the female body and the effeminate male. However, while white masculinities are envisioned, situated and maintained as benevolent, sexually desirable and measured patriarchs, black masculinities are marked as dangerous, hyper-sexual, erratic and animalistic in our white supremacist, heterosexist, patriarchal-capitalist society. This demarcation of the black male as an uncontrollable yet attractive, nuisance births the socio-legal logic necessary for state-control of black bodies male—and by extension black women, girls and children—through various social, political, legal and extrajudicial apparatus and phenomenon, creating a collective indifference and communal shrug when black boys and men are routinely killed, discarded and swooped up by the state in jails, prisons and community supervision. Black access to patriarchy is not a solution—indeed it is a dangerous trick and empty enticement to join a burning house—but its consequences have interesting and violent impacts. Because cisheteropatriarchy is the fulcrum of American society, its logic not only polices the imaginative and reality of the household but also power distribution. Power in the United States is filtered through the male—as the imagined economic and political power center of a household—this has tragic implications for black people. The reality of the black family is not a consideration of white patriarchy or feminisms. The archetypical portrait of a nuclear, upper-middle class family with a working man and a woman who works in the house—or more moderately—two privately employed caregivers does not capture the reality of black, single and dual parent, working and middle class families. Because black men are seen as a natural nuisance, it inevitably becomes the job of the white supremacist state to provide a sense of order, calm and control and it does so through its indiscriminate policing and slaying of black boys, men, bois, girls and gurls. Patriarchy would grant this power to violate to the man, modern feminisms to all people and a humanist politic, to no one at all.

In Black heterosexist spaces black masculinities are often constructed similarly to white masculinities. They are the desirable patriarchs, the locusts of power. Where the white supremacist gaze posits black male sexual virility and general power as dangerous mutations, the black gaze notes them as points of pride, if not necessary characteristics for survival where one is constantly battling white supremacist, capitalistic machinery for humanization and access to sociopolitical resources, goods and services. This is our yearning for equality, our performance of self-worth, we too can wield power—we say. This reverence and longing for the omnipotent, omniscient black patriarch–situated and proved by his masculinity–often obscures or erases the role of the left of masculine, and/or BlaQueer male, and completely obliterates the central role and power of black womyn. Access to, and performance of, these romanticized, deified notions of black masculinity function as a method of gatekeeping. Those who fail, or decide not to, display the pre-authorized script are marked as in-authentic, insufficiently black-male and, often, a threat to real black maleness, the black family and blackness writ large. This reality births the liminal space that BlaQueer men must navigate. We are neither white nor the traditional black patriarch yet our safety, sanity and success is measured and threatened by (in)access to both. This necessitates the creation of a space for other brothers, brothers like us.

The importance, emergence and longevity of BlaQueer, male spaces has been documented in works such as "Paris is Burning" and the artistry, poetry and essays of historic and modern griots such as: Essex Hemphill, Joseph Beam, James Baldwin, Kenyon Farrow, Dr. Jafari Allen, Dr. E. Patrick Johnson, Dr. Marlon Bailey, Rotemi Fani-Kayode and many others. But do these spaces need to be specifically or normatively male? Is that not another learned—if not robotic—routine that removes us further from self and deeper into a trance of racial-sexual performatives? From slave-ships and auction blocks to ballrooms and barber shops, BlaQueer folks have long-established and maintained spaces of relative safety, affirmation and fuller existences. Masculine anxiety, homo-antagonism, femme-phobia, trans-genocides, and white supremacy have necessitated the creation of alternative communities and spaces, lest we forfeit portions of ourselves and circumcise the components of our realities. These spaces provide a home to a diaspora of diasporas. They allow for safe(r) exploration of sexualities, (non)genders and notions of queerness and blackness, allowing for those pushed to the margins to exist and thrive at the center of their own world. While these spaces provide an undeniable layer of protection for its residents, to understand them as a simple reaction to violence—for a sanctuary from it—would be both misguided and incomplete.

BlaQueer communities are a fertile birthing place r/evolutionary existences and creativity; complete with new languages, phrases and ideologies that connect, unpack and dissect seemingly disparate realities, circumstances and politics. BlaQueer folk are griots, translators, pedagogues, artists, healers, lovers, activists and truth-seekers. They are fashionistas, writers, speakers, bloggers and creators. They work with their hearts, hands, minds and bodies. Our bodies are central locations of conversation, meaning-making and perfect imperfections. In short, BlaQueer people are a cosmos, affected but not contained by the bounds neither blackness or queerness. In the words of Whitman, we are vast and contain multitudes. We are masters, servants and queens of the in-betweens. We have perfected liminal existences, particularly those between and beyond masculinity and femininity, into an art. We have moved beyond coining positive terms for, and promoted acceptance of, left of masculine and femme men. We are in the process of noting that masculinity and femininity are prisons of performance, while also noting and recollecting their real and lived effects and our freedoms to dance as we please. While much work remains in the full acceptance and celebration of femme, GenderQueer, ButchQueen and Trans* folk, due to our continued internalized (sexual) masculine-anxiety, our community spaces are becoming places where we can and do flourish, thrive and move beyond mere survival. We are birthing a new BlaQueer love and power practice. But can masculinity, with its violent tendencies, be counted among the welcomed multitudes of our cosmic existences?

How do we contend with the hegemonic role of masculinity in society writ large, while also noting how access to femininity, or social, physical and verbal performance of the so-called "feminine" (see: tea, beat-faces, shade, walks, style,"girl" and "sis") might function or be read as safer entry points to authenticity in BlaQueer—as opposed to Black Gay— spaces? Those of us who identity as Femme, Queen, GenderQueer, ButchQueen and Trans* have had our identity violently branded onto our flesh. For better and for worse, we are not called to assert or prove our queerness, but instead our humanity, a sick twist on othered predicament. Our identities have long-standing herstories and communities within BlaQueer spaces. To be clear, these spaces are not sites of privilege, but outposts of refuge. We birthed them not out of desire but necessity. For us, our familial homes are often where the hatred is. However, the same cannot be said for masculine men, for myriad reasons. Their type of other is often seen as too normative to be queer, too privileged to need community and too violent to be close. While we cannot deny the power and privilege of masculine performance in society—nor can we discount the internal and external physical, emotional and legal violence that originates from masculine ideologies—we must analyze whether and how this changes in our spaces. Masculine men too, suffer from the violence of masculine privilege and its requirements for internal dehumanization. Daily they perform, internalize and circumcise themselves to play the role, perfectly, silently and with suicidal ease. The overtly masculine gay or bisexual male is often read as a temporary or probationary community-member at best and marked as Trade, Down Low or confused. These markers have the effect of erasing their queer existences, obscuring access to a queer identity and practice while resurrecting antiquated tropes about black, male sexualities rooted in racial-sexual terrors, historic and present. This type of authenticity-checking relegates performances of masculinity, and proximity to it, as desirable (sexually), alien (due to in-access to aforementioned community/cultural markers) and threatening (sociopolitically).

Taken in context, an aversion to, and skepticism of, masculinity is understandable, if not necessary for our protection. It has been purposed again and again as a bludgeon against queer people of color. In order to perfect our community, we must answer a few questions. Do we wish to be a discursive, radical culture that creates a safe(r) space for all BlaQueer folks? Can one be simultaneously masculine, bio-male and queer? Can masculinity be queer? Or is it simply a reflection of patriarchal power and desire structures? Alternatively, is the "femme-ish," dominant portrayal of queer, people of color culture(s), identities and spaces an inversion of masculine privilege; where incidental access to femininity or the ability to gender/code-switch or perform is a requisite, privilege or passport required for queer-authenticity, marking fluidity as a form of (sub)cultural power? This is not to say that being femme is a privilege, it is often a death sentence, but to question how we read signals of gender performance and which, if any power, violence, fluidity or permissions we assign to it. We must question and note how power is moving, where it resides, whether its present and specific function is problematic and if so, should we care? Finally, we must question the effects of power, through the role of femininities, masculinities and gender fucking in the birthing, perversion, strangling and maintenance of restorative, healing and liberatory BlaQueer communities.

I have yet to determine whether BlaQueerness is expansive enough to include both masculinities and femininities without inspiring or permitting friction or a continuation the masculine privilege exerted in the American, heterosexist, cispatriarchal society. Rather, I question if we should drop the masculine-feminine, performance identification system all together and imagine a deeper freedom. I posit that it is not only the role, but the nature of BlaQueerness to mark, encourage, celebrate and translate the flows of the myriad existences and performances of our selves. We are a diaspora that is fine-tuned for imaginative reconstruction, hopeful reconciliation and complex and compounded existences. In our blood, one will find a chorus of contradictory narratives, truths, performances and existences that map and center the margins of our his/her/ourstories. Just as our bodies have made peace with warring pieces of ourselves, our community is called to continually become whole, reclaiming our cosmic existence as an inarticulable juggernaut of perfect, imperfections. In order to create and maintain true liberation, we must discard the master, the tools and his houses and begin the work of complete divestment.

Black Lives Matter: Re-centering Blackness Unbound, Noting White Terrorism & Shutting Shit Down

Co-written with Jonathan Jacob Moore Delia Younge

"Sometimes people try to destroy you, precisely because they recognize your power–not because they don't see it, but because they see it and they don't want it to exist."

-Bell Hooks

Whiteness knows that Black lives matter; that's the starting point. They been done peeped that. They peeped that during slavery and kept us as property because we have been, and always will be the basis of white wealth, value, purpose and power. They created the Black Codes to keep Blackness bound, because just a few years of Reconstruction showed that the perverse feelings, fears and gaze of whiteness was nothing but gasoline on the fire of a black survival practice that swept up coin, resources and reaffirmed Black humanity, intelligence, grit, love and survivorship. It served as a means to keep us bound in the need for acceptance once more. Black women launched a domestic campaign post-Reconstruction to 'clean house,' the beginnings of the stronghold of respectability politics. It begged whiteness to gaze upon what they thought could be washed over. It was the type of campaign that pitted blackness against blackness, as not everyone could be part of a movement that as Lorde warned us (and it rings true today even before she said it) would always fail to accomplish its goals because of the rusted, trapped nature of its tools.

One could argue that the dehumanization, commodification, and enslavement of Black peoples constitutes an unparalleled crime against humanity. Consequently, the resilience borne out of these histories remain the most powerful threat to the racial status quo in the United States and White supremacy worldwide. They know that Black lives matter. Their very existence is predicated on this knowledge as fact and this knowledge as an "unknown". But we know better. They knew Black lives matter, through and true, during Jim Crow and the creation of the modern Black Codes (prison industrial complex, inequitable enforcement, criminalization of poverty and non-culture), so they created policy regimes that birthed and reared a separate Black reality–a de facto Black America bonded through racialized living conditions–marked, maimed, lashed and stereotyped by behavior (read:'survival practices) necessary in order to defeat corporeal death through these animalistic torture and hazing practices (bombings, scientific tests, drug drops, military grade police violence and drive-bys, assassinations). They systematically attempted to kill us by stealing our faith in God, science, state, police and home as guardians of our safety, our humanity, the sense that our Black lives could matter, not even to us. Only whiteness could protect or redeem us. We remain unconvinced.

They know that Black lives matter. Indeed, that all Black lives matter. They are watching you and I. They been woke. After all, this nation is the home of white supremacist, heterosexist, patriarchal, capitalistic, imperialist rule…and we are expected to perform as its humble servants; always serving, perhaps surviving, never living, freely. For want of a gaze we end up bodies hanging, bodies lying–dead, with a contagion of paralysis. When we appeal to them or shake the chandeliers to show ourselves and be seen and affirmed, we may do a work of having a life that matters–like a fly that buzzes to announce its presence–but only because they said so. When the buzz becomes a distraction, a swatter is always at arms-length. When Black people find themselves as worthy of love, safety, or even oxygen, we are dealt with as the threats we are. When we position the existence of our humanity upon the persistence of the white gaze, we allow our lives to flash in the blink of an unbothered eye. Perhaps we might add an addendum to a worthy mantra: Black lives matter to us, and now white terrorism and exploitation will have consequences. We do not, and have never, toiled for their gaze, approval or attention for authentication. I am because you are, we are because the Cosmos had a sense of fairness to this world. When Baldwin wrote on the uses of the blues, it was about the power we can claim in life that they cannot use or abuse because they do not understand it. It has never been about whether or not Black lives forgive whiteness for its history of erasure, but rather about whiteness' ongoing need to have us long for its gaze and acceptance, in chains economic, psychosocial and extrajudicial. We do not shuck and jive for white tears. We shut shit down until structures stand for the maintenance of our liberation. If they do not stand, we can no longer afford to mourn their fall. This is the last curtain call.

These are the spaces we choose to exist in. We are making these and reshaping them daily. We are reshaping our world in the process. We must use them to gather together all who are living, to make them woke to this reality, these realities, and a part of the liberatory body as well. This is the work of building through love and communal support. By re-centering blackness, BlaQueerness and black womynhood into the power and humanity of black hands, black love, and black spaces, we find liberation. We know our worth as a masterpiece, an intimate thing that does not need to hang against pale-white walls to be seen, to be felt, to be beautiful. We do not need to hang to be beautiful. We must meet pleas for enlightenment with demands for revolutionary and system-shattering honesty-to be less invested in the inoperable American surgery of "making" Black life "matter" and more invested in revealing the ignorance as myth and White denial of knowing as a deadly force, is indeed a noble decree. We will no longer be circumcised by the dull scalpel of whiteness unleashed. So next time we shut shit down, and indeed we must, we shall make all parties aware–black, brown and white, white supremacists-terrorists alike–it's about us. It's the terrorism, boo.

The Delusion of Non-Violence

There is no such thing as non-violence.

Violence is when the police kill our children.

Tamir

That is violence.

Violence is when are expected, implored and allowed to March and sing and pray, peacefully.

Realize The Dream.

Violence lurks. Can't you smell it? Feel it festering under your nose? That wound that exists in your soul is the result of a violent blow.

There is violence in the land, it appears even in our gaze. It resides in the terror exacted on a community, when motherless children and childless mothers see the state-endorsed killers marauding justice with tax-paid badges, that's violence.

ChIraq

Violence is the smile and commentary you are supposed to give the mayor for a faux investigation you fought for. That is violence.

LaQuan

Violence is the role and responsibility inscribed upon your body, as the "rational" voice of black survivors and bereaved folks, lest the badges, bullets and death squads return. That is violence.

The Martin Family

Violence is the realization that the same entity that killed your son, caged your brother, harassed you and profiles your sister…is who answers the phone when your life is in jeopardy. That is violence.

Sisters Miriam Carey, Yvette Smith, Shelly Frey, Darnisha Harris, Malissa Williams, Alesia Thomas, Shantel Davis, Rekia Boyd, Shereese Francis, Aiyana Stanley-Jones, Tarika Wilson, Kathryn Johnston, Alberta Spruill, Kendra James

Violence is knowing that another boy, girl, boi, gurl, man, womyn, trans*/GNC/NB person is being killed, harassed or ignored by the police as you court peace. That is violence.

Womyn: Ty Underwood, Lamia Beard, Yazmin Vash Payne, Taja Gabrielle DeJesus, Penny Proud, Bri Golec, Kristina Gomez Reinwald, Keyshia Blige, Maya Hall, London Chanel, Mercedes Williamson, Shade Schuler, India Clarke, Ashton O'Hara, Amber Monroe, Kandis Capri, Elisha Walker, Tamara Dominguez, Kiesha Jenkins, Zella Ziona

Shit ain't peaceful and it ain't cute.

Amerikkka,

Goddamn.

Privilege, Queerness & Other Myths From The Master

Different iterations of the concepts in this essay appeared at BlaQueerFlow, then at Gawker, as "Black Gay Privilege: Racial-Sexual Terror Unmasked" and "The Truth About Black Gay Privilege," respectively. While related, this essay includes important interventions, additional insights and much more critical in its analysis.

Black gay privilege has often been articulated as a special benefit enjoyed by black gay men. This 'privilege' supposedly enables us to evade the traditional economic and racial dominations experienced by (straight) black men and produced by white anxiety and white supremacy. The crux of the argument is such: white people are less intimidated by black gay men, because they are seen as less of a threat. Therefore, black gay men enjoy greater employment options and benefits than black straight men, and perhaps, straight black women. It is a straight-forward argument. Said 'privilege' is situated on the assertion that black gay men are less masculine—less black—and therefore less intimidating to white men and women and more likely to be hired and promoted. The threat is not one simply born of queerness, but rather one situated in the assumed de-blackening effect of non-heterosexual existences. There are many problems with this assertion, but let us first begin with the obvious.

Neither Queerness nor same-sex attraction inherently require or guarantee a particular performance of masculinities, femininities or blacknesses. First, we must begin to under the fundamental differences between same-sex attraction, or being gay, from that of Queerness. Same-sex at-

158

traction, or being gay, is simply that: same sex attraction, with a desire for inclusion. It is a passively apolitical existence that positions itself as twin of a cisheteropatriarchal life and love practices, situating power in the dominant male body, and only differentiated by the ways in which it performs sexual and gender violence—normatively anal, as opposed to vaginal. Notions of manhood, domestic power divisions and the quest for patriarchal, socioeconomic domination remain the same. In many ways modern gay realities and perhaps new-feminisms are neoliberal capitalisms dipped in marginalized dialectics. While there is certainly nothing wrong with wanting to be treated like a human being--pay equity, marriage equality, gender equality and tax issues--there is something wrong our notion when our notion of humanity is based off the archetypical white, social mobile, (upper) middle-class male. In many cases, we have started to demand is equal access to cisheteropatriarchy, equal access to the fruits and blood of capitalisms, equal access to imperialism. In contrast, Queer & Feminists politics cannot be about becoming (hu)man. Instead, they must be about the undoing and unbecoming of categorical—racial, gender, sexual, class, national, ethnic, religious—existences that are enforced, incentivized, naturalized and lashed by myriad power structures (state, family and self). Queer and Feminist politics, people and practices do and must strive for the liberation of the human soul, free from the iron hot cultural brands on the minds, bodies and spirits free-born peoples. They must be about redefining what humanity is, providing an alternative for what we could be and creating roadmaps to freedom from patriarchy, capitalisms, state and racial-sexual terrorisms. I have no problem with equality, but lets not call it justice. It's simply access.

This is equally true for heterosexual black men. Their access to employment and wealth accumulation, across gender performance, should not be seen as privilege but simply entry to a capitalistic system that requires a pound of black humanity as levy. In this capitalistic system, or socioeconomic pyramid scheme, racial-sexual discriminatory hiring (and firing) practices are not a function of the sexual practices or gender performances of black men, but instead a display of white (masculine) anxieties and insecurities and the nature of radicalized capitalisms. These systems of power and wealth maldistribution depend on a caste of underpaid and undervalued peoples, whether permanent or fluid, to perform the base of the pyramid. They are foundational to the existence of society and the sustained value of capital, yet they are denigrated, because if their value is realized internally, they might be externally liberated and destroy the system and ideology that profits from their open-air prison. Therefore, those that benefit most from structural power and inequity, exist with an external angst about their unnatural positions of influence and wealth accumulation. These insecurities and anxieties are similarly rooted in racial-sexual and gender tropes imputed on black bodies during slavery. Black male and female bodies—across sex, sexuality and gender performance—were routinely violated in circus-like displays of racial-sexual terrors. These white family events included lynching, penectomies, breast augmentation and genital mutilations—whereby the black body would be photographed, embalmed and mailed across the nation as part and parcel of the erotic, communal practice of white redemption. These events occurred for myriad, sadistic reasons, but most often functioned as violent lessons of racial-sexual comportment. The official word, that black men and women were hyper-sexual and needed to be punished, eliminated and made examples of, was held as gospel in the white community–and widely disputed amongst black survivors. The activist and scholar Ida B. Wells noted that most were terrorized not for their sexual proclivities but for their refusal to be used for the sexual pleasure of slaveholders, male and female, gay and straight. In short, black people were killed not for acts of sexual violence, but sexual resistance, interpreted as violence to the system of white racial-sexual power and domination. This was a frontal assault on white anxieties—sexual, racial, economic and spiritual—and for the sake of nation, for the sake of white supremacist ideology, for whiteness to remain superior, the specter of the powerful black body required dismemberment. In layman's terms, they wanted to teach (read: force) black people how to (sexually) act (read: submit) through blood, sport and the erotic.

The phenomena of some black gay men accessing professional longevity is not about privilege. Privilege is an unearned benefit, bestowed without merit. This is different. This is survival jujitsu. This—the forced circumcision of blackness from queerness, and queerness from masculinities—in order to remain employed is violence, racial-sexual terror and psychological genocide. Gay, bisexual, queer and same-gender loving black men exist in a space socially and politically apart from heterosexual

161

black men–we are the other brothers, a scourge on a discouraged peoples. Daily we are forced to choose and navigate if, how and when we perform maleness, in order to affirm our identity and preserve our safety from patriarchal violence from brothers and sisters alike. We are also called and required to police our blackness in a way that allows us to remain close to home and family, while also allowing proximity to whiteness as sociocultural capital/property, to avert or lessen white supremacist violence. Finally we must navigate, customize and reform our queerness, second by second, to avert heterosexist violence, obscure our seemingly dangerous blackness and assert our power as men–that is, the power to avert systemic (cis) male-domination, visited on the bodies of all women. Put simply, BlaQueerness is the practice of the survival of racial-sexual circumcisions, a two-step of terror-evasion and all too often, gendered-terror reproduction.

"To be a Negro in this country and to be relatively conscious is to be in a rage almost all the time."

-James Baldwin

When we are coerced to perform, mask and other our personal performances of us—whether blackness, black maleness, Gender Non-Conforming, Trans* or BlaQueer–in order to evade a layer of white su-

premacist violence and anxieties, we enable ourselves to climb socioeco-
nomic ladders, however frail, to financial sociopolitical wealth. However
in doing so we commit to reifying and endorsing the work and will of
white supremacy, corporeal capitalism and cisheteropatriarchy through our
assent. We then end up compromising ourselves and our right and abilities
to simply be, us, alive: existing in nature. This isn't privilege. It's survival
jujitsu. It's debilitating. It is genocide. We are placed in the impossible po-
sition of negotiating between survival under white supremacy, and hunger
within personal black (queer) authenticity.

The notion of black gay "privilege"–aside from erasing the reali-
ties of "right of masculine" gay men, trans men and womyn–positions the
BlaQueer as a buffer between white supremacists hiring practices and their
black critics. The logic goes, because we hired these black men, white su-
premacists note, we cannot be racist. Lost in translation is the requirement
of BlaQueer folk to mortgage control of their bodies, lease their humanity,
and performances of self to their employer as a precondition of employ-
ment. Also lost is the implicit messages that either these (BlaQueer) men
are ideal and preferable and/or other black men are deficient by choice or
nature. This enables race, and by extension power, to be evaded as the fo-
cal point and instead posits responsibility on the deficiency of black,
straight, masculine presenting men and ire on seemingly unearned position
of the BlaQueer.

"The power of the white world is threatened whenever

a black man refuses to accept the white world's definitions."

-James Baldwin

There is no black gay privilege. There are white supremacist, heterosexist, patriarchal, capitalistic anxieties engraved upon black, gay bodies, through violent hiring, firing, recruitment and retention practices. There is violence–psychological and psychosocial terrorisms–in forced, perverted performances of our selves, in order to find a sweet spot between masculinities and femininities that do not arouse white fear, white guilt or white notions of equity. We are to be propertied–seen, heard and felt as accessible and owned by employers for their pleasure and fulfillment. Our given role then, in this system, is to do what the ideology of cisheteropatriarchal, capitalistic, ableist, white supremacy authenticates as "straight" or "masculine" black men, will not: swallow micro-aggressions, violences and inequity with a smile and a hair-flip. Unfortunately for the aforementioned system, BlaQueer men and womyn are the kings and queens of subversive existences, politics and liberatory practices.

"If a human chain

can be formed

around missiles sites

then surely black men

can form human chains

around Anacostia, Harlem

South Africa, Wall Street

Hollywood, each other.

If we have to take tomorrow with our own blood,

are we ready? ....

All I want to know for my own protection is,

are we ready for whatever,

whenever?"

-Essex Hemphill

Yes, yes we are. We must use the insights and lessons of the scars of oppression, to draw and map our home to collective freedom and liberations. There is no cure, no panacea, no treatment to the rage and resolve imbedded within the bones of BlaQueer peoples, outside of Black and BlaQueer liberations. We are not the ones we've been waiting for. We are the ones we have been loving for, dying for, and living for. We do this in remembrance of our ancestors, in humanization of ourselves and the hope of those coming next. We are ready, we are willing and we will win.

Fucked By God's Queer('d) Scalpel!

Psalm 34: Praising, Hazing & God(less) Circumcisions

34 *I will bless the Lord at all times: his praise shall continually be in my mouth.*

My mouth was once a vessel of the black prophetic tradition. My voice bellowed the goodness of the deliverer, the way maker, the mighty load carrier until I was promised that my load might be too much to ask of God. Preacher boy I was, queer boy I was(n't), at the pulpit. I spent many years deep in the closet, fearing myself, fearing God, seeking myself, seeking God under the weight–errr covering–of my Pastor; suffocating, being saved. I wept, I fasted, I prayed for mercy, for death, for AIDS, for love, for family, for judgement; so that His praise could be in my mouth and not be unclean. Preacher boy, I was, queer boy I was(n't)..at the pulpit on Sundays I preached a word of enlightenment…an image of the Light of God…a god that I prayed existed in a loving glory in contrast to that of the angry old white man that my angry black Pastor preached would send red fire down onto brown bodies if we didn't stop our descent into Soddam and Gomorrahesque debauchery…loving each other…black men..loving each other..that was a sin..better to load my pistol and take life..than to feed a brother my heart..or my life-force..and suck seed..succeed together. My mouth couldn't contain his praise..not at all…because my times didn't mesh right, my clock was off..so I blessed him with tithes and offerings..to never return to his presence..if only we'd respect each other's space..a truce.

2 *My soul shall make her boast in the Lord: the humble shall hear thereof, and be glad.*

Boasted I did. Freshman year I started a bible club at school. 5am every morning I led an international prayer call with similarly afflicted brothers. We were the sons of Paul…but our thorn was different. Not different like those white boys with skinny jeans, limp wrists, rolled joints and high pitches. Na…we were black and queer and we had flow. BlaQueerflow. We slide through the boundaries of race, sex, gender, sexuality and class with the class and precision of newest Chi-Town Step. We were raised right..to trust in the Lord with all our hearts. So we prayed. Anywhere between 5-20 BlaQueer men with flow…across the country. We met on sites like Hi5, BlackGayChatLive, Tagged..we loved each other. We prayed and wept, every morning..long-distance..around 5am so we could use free minutes. By 6:30am, I had a sermonette ready for my bible club of 20+ mostly white kids waiting to hear my preacher voice. Holy T, Bible Brother, Prayer Warrior, Elder Wilson, that was me, they said. I was glad, mostly, now I had a holy-ish name. But my holy oil could never soothe the itch within my soul. I wanted Him in me. But I also wanted him, Brian, too. My crush. With butter-brown skin, just shade lighter than mine, like color of sweet potato pie. Big lips, so soft, like mine. He could dance, he was witty, he was an athlete, he was going places, like me. Going to hell too, just like me. but nobody knew about us but us. He was scared as fuck. Word. Me too. We couldn't talk about it, his lips made me smile and freed me. He was the first to taste my honey. I hope it was sweet. Our lips weren't made for secrets…So I boasted…about God. Because everyone could hear that, and it made momma proud..and maybe I'd get out of hell. I did believe.

3 *O magnify the Lord with me, and let us exalt his name together.*

There was no pretending. My tears were real that day, all those days, at the altar. I didn't get this acne on purpose! Hands laid, spit flying, blessed oil pouring from my scalp to my pores. I screamed to Jesus. I jumped. I ran. I shouted. I spoke in tongues. I rolled…on the floor..with the punches…between the pastor's bigoted but heartfelt prayers and speeches and warnings…and over the church mothers long-discarded heals and falling weaves, I tried. I cried…for my mother because I knew that when she died we would not be reunited…for siblings because we only had this fucked up life together and it had to count…we were hungry, cold, abandoned, struggling and just had each other with no lights or toys to depend on..and we fought too much..but I wouldn't see them in the afterlife either because I didn't choose to leave it for this gay sex thing. I'd never had sex, not that I could remember…really. That was violence, he gave that to me, took it from me... That shit can't be spoken, not in God's house. It's not "biblical" as they say.

4 *I sought the Lord, and he heard me, and delivered me from all my fears.*

And one day I ran. The Church of God in Christ had been home, not like my house…no electricity, drugged out mom, food gone, hungry little siblings, beer bottles piled..brandy..crack heads…nameless men/suitors/players/tricks..and the reminder that I was 15 and working 30 hours a week. I ran…into books…into work…into dreams of success and freedom from the cycle of intergenerational poverty and internal hate. I cut ties from the Church because it only taught me suicide..despite providing benefits to sustain my physical body (food, conversation, clothes, heat, water). I had to begin to hate who I was being defined as. I didn't want to rule over women, especially not black women. My grandmother was not my equal, she was superior. My sister was going to be even more powerful than her. I was a man with feelings. I enjoyed poetry as much as, or more than, basketball or football. I wasn't angry, I was curious. I had no interest in being the head of anyone's household or having children. Their definition of me was one of a misogynist, patriarchal, heterosexist, nativist, white supremacist negro..who took orders..purportedly from the bible, while never reading enough to be intelligible or critical. I knew I had to run. So I left to New Mexico to look at myself.

5 They looked unto him, and were lightened: and their faces were not ashamed.

They saw me as I began to: BlaQueer and full of life. They…from countries all over the world..smiled and I smiled back, with my lips, with my heart and I hugged myself. I hugged my blackness. I hugged my queerness. I hugged my poverty. I loved it. I fell in love with myself…and a boy..and got my heart broken..and gained a best friend. And..then…it almost ended as quickly as it began..they tried to Assata me. I almost died..

8 O taste and see that the Lord is good: blessed is the man that trusteth in him.

And now I'm coming home. A brilliant professor of mine once told that for many of us "home is where the hatred is." Word. Scripture. Truth. Fact. So i'm exiting the master's house and making a home "not made by man's hand." My prayer is best encapsulated by the old gospel song "Lord Keep Me Day by Day." I no longer desire survival but a life of giving, of living, of producing love and loving spaces and that is only possible through the production of a healing space…a home. That home for me is about accessing and creating that which cannot be explained, said or named. It is about creating realities that we all desire but have yet to co-produce. It is about employing, sharing and articulating the love of the creator in a way that creates and sustains souls long since maimed by our/ their/my since of unbelonging. So this journey, this home-going, isn't about returning to the Church of God in Christ..or any physical church space for that matter..but instead a returning the notion of communal love and beginning to re-acknowledge the divine that exists within us all. I've recommitted myself to seeing the world with a child eyes and loving with a heart who knows it's purpose to give and receive equally, even when love doesn't seem forthcoming or possible, for the sake of my own humanity. This home is carried with me everywhere I go. There have been growing pains, but for once, the space evolves to house me instead of my body being circumcised to crouch into the space.

The (Ultimate) Trade: Getting to BlaQueer Realities

Momma's love child is what she called me. She said it with joy and pride, but her eyes could never lie to mine. Big, dark brown with an almond hint that only that you could see if you were close enough to me–my eyes were her pride and joy. I was her man-child. She warned me about the danger of those eyes, full of mystery and intrigue, and their impending danger, waiting to break the hearts of young girls. I never wanted girls. I was a child of women. I was raised by women. I loved women. Free women, full women, Black women, full of color. Full breasted, thick waists, strong arms and rhythmic thighs..those were the places I took refuge as a frightened and growing child. A black boy looking, knowing that home rested somewhere in the bodies of black women. Noting could reach me there. But I didn't want them in that way. No, not sexually. No, it would be a violation. I loved black women. I could not do the things that my uncles, (fore)father(s), cousins and kin folk had done. I could never hurt them. The thought pained me. Sex was pain. Good never came of it.

I told Pastor this. He tried to convince me that my "affliction of the flesh"–my love of men–was due to my fatherless upbringing. He was implying that there was a deficiency in the women of my life, they lacked the power-resolve of a man, therefore allowing this "spirit of homosexuality" to arise within me. My face burned. I did not know whether homosexuality, as he called it, was a demon, it was not my real concern. I was upset that he had insulted my mothers, grandmothers, aunts, cousins, kinfolk; calling them a failure, calling me their failure, marking those strong, thick bodies as inadequate. Had he not seen the power of their faces, deflecting insult and empty promises without blinking? Had he never felt their love in a season of pain? Did he even *know any* Black women-folk? In that moment I willed myself into loving my queerness, or at least beginning the journey. In that moment, at 15 or 16, I linked my authentic demonstration and commitment to self-love as a reflection of my love of the work of the women that came before me. The Pastor had implicitly asked me to trade my pride of the women who had reared for a deep shame, he wanted to trade my burgeoning feminism with a desire for heteropatriarchy and misogyny. My stomach hurt. It was as if he had reached into my chest, down to my bowels and begin to twist and squeeze my intestines. I was angry, violated, paralyzed and distraught. I ran from his office, from his church, from his covering, into the arms of my grandmother.

I had begun to accept my queerness because my grandmother had long ago planted a resilient seed of self-love within me. Every morning that I woke, and every night before I slept, she would summon me to her bosom, caress my cheeks and remind that "I love you forever, and ever and always" just before kissing me on the cheek and bidding me good-night or good morning. The love of a black woman is stronger than the self-hate of a black boy, especially when consistent. There is something

175

invincible and enduring about that type of love. It envelopes you. It dares you to submit. Black men don't like to lose dares. It enveloped me and brought me from the brink of disrepair. She knew I wasn't simply gay, but queer, my politic was emerging. I had long ago disavowed gender-based expectations of me–I could braid, cornrow, dye, perm, curl and cut hair much better than all of my cousins and many of my aunts. I jumped rope. I boxed. I was a track and field and football champion. I loved to dance, sing and act. I recited Malcolm without prompting. Maya Angelou was my favorite. Prince, Michael, Janet, Whitney, Maxwell, Snoop, Ice Cube, Tupac and Nas: those were my favorite artists. I was a poet. I loved my long hair, especially curled. I was also a great shot. I had a quick temper with white boys–they feared me. I kicked ass. I was gentle with people of color–I could see and sense our collective pain–sometimes I would be completely still and silent, just to bask in our togetherness. I relished the black man's nod as a cultural-spiritual experience of the highest order.

I loved being black. I was embracing my queer affect. I was not ready to be a black man though. I feared black men. I loved them for a distance, but they were dangerous. They had violated my mother, my aunts, my cousins, my grandmothers. They were to be loved. They deserved love. But, you "couldn't trust em' as far you could throw em.'" They always had some little trick it seemed. They'd make you love them, grow comfortable and just as soon as you closed your eyes, you'd find your heart flip-flopping on the ground like a fish out of water, struggling for air, looking a hot, damn mess. You'd taken the bait and it wasn't even your first time being hooked. Grandma Rose always said, *"A dog that brings a bone carries a bone."* So much trouble. It seemed to reside deep within them. I looked like them. I had all their features. Thick, soft, full lips. Deep brown eyes and long lashes. I was slim and muscular, a natural athlete. Witty, to a fault, with a winning smile and thick, enduring hair that protected me from the sun. It scared me. I was beautiful. I loved myself. I knew I was a piece of art. But..I didn't want to be like them. I didn't want to cause pain, so I ran. I became Tabias, the anti-normative black man. I was a "new black" in my little brain, before I woke up.

But then I was taken into handcuffs. Slammed on the ground. Lips bleeding. 16 years old. Handcuffs tight around my wrists. We were driving across town the first time, going 29 in a 30. Caught. Speed trap. We–Jerry, Nick, Denzell–my two best friends and my younger cousin, looked dangerous. We were put in jail. Our parents were called. Curfew violation, in the town with no curfew. The next time I was protesting the death penalty– the officer asked me if I wanted to know what the electric chair felt like. Word. I was less afraid of dying this time, because I was beginning to live. They had already killed my cousin Quendell. Let him choke on his own vomit. Mysterious deaths. Black boys killed, before they leave home. Black men mortally wounded, become they make homes. I was young, gifted, queer and black. I wasn't wounded. I was dangerous. I knew it. They knew it. I knew that they knew it. I became a black, queer man, unafraid of the str8 fuckers who would shame me by day and attempt to (be) fuck(ed) (by) me at night. I was amused. I thought white boys feared me and lived for my gaze. I later realized I was simply a walking porno in their screenplay, a fuck scene they became obsessed with but were never qualified to unravel, understand or experience. Sex with white boys was a particular type of therapy–I gave them my rage, roughly, through complete domination–they loved it, not knowing I hated them back then. I loved one, he was amazing. A true lover, with an uncanny ability to illuminate and prove my humanity and my ability to love and be loved. Until he broke, first himself, then the rupture of love ethics began..and I re-met myself as a lover of men of color. No boys. No white supremacists. Not simply men of pigmentation, but men of color. Men who were about living in color, with colored folks, no fucks given, unless it was for the struggle or liberation. Men who made my brain hard and gave me wisdom with their lips, love through their hips and sex through their acts of care. It was a mind fuck. First Latinos–Puerto Ricans–then Palestinians–then black men. Dominicans. Black men. Men that are black. Brothers. Lovers. Homie. Lover. Friends. I learned to have homies, lovers and friends. Black as night, brown as mahogany. Skin blended and interwined, not knowing ends or beginnings. Love and loving bodies..no objectification. Loving, bodies being loved, loved bodies, love on bodies, caresses, kisses, affirmation. Affirming caresses, Loving kisses, kisses of love. Feminist, Queer, Black sex. No fucking. Just sex. Sapiosexual homosexuals. Versatility. Stress free. Nirvana.

It was a barter. A trade. A win. You can have your racial-sexual terror, your cisheteropatriarchy, your respectability politics, your "real black men," jockin' "new black" politics, masculinity-jockin', trade-boys, your "no fat-femmes-out-asians-vers-poz-tranny-diseased" fuckery. I'll take them all. Give me a poz, butchqueen who gives no fucks about the way the world reads her/his/their/zhe body, but instead reads you their essence, their tattoos, their survival tactics, with grace, drama and grit. It was a trade. A trade of prisons for power. A trade of fuckery for freedom. A trade of languishing existences for loving praxis. A trade of white supremacy for un-adultered, liberated BlaQueeRealness. It was a trade and I won.

The Politics of Accessibility: Love, Work & Survival Schemes

It never made much sense to me. I mean, don't get me wrong. I had grown up with little and learned the worth of a quarter, fuck a dollar. I knew how to work hard. I valued hard work. I had to work hard to survive. Four quarters meant a loaf of starch white bread, grab another eight quarters and you could get a pound of bologna and a spot of miracle whip. Fried up, flipped and spread you had a meal. I knew how to work hard. I knew the struggle of acquiring scraps, let alone sustenance. I know how to how work hard. I know the costs, the hunger pains, the callous hands and hearts. But who the fuck wants that shit? Who wants to work hard? To what end?

Struggle porn. It has to be struggle porn. Struggling folks glorifying the site and sight of pain, their ability to endure it, in order to valorize it, infuse honor into it, decorate the load. That's what folks are doing when they ask if I have a "real" job. As if law school, freelance writing, public speaking and community organizing/educating aren't real. Na, it's not that my work is a figment of their–or my–imagination, it's that it is out of the realm of what is normal, what has connected us. It infuses no honor on what we've overcome, endured and still survive/live. The struggle—corporeal capitalisms—is moved from eyesore and sight of clear trauma, to an un-lubricated fuck by the biggest of sociopolitical dicks. It becomes an honor to take it all, without a whimper, without slick, efficient preparation. Everyone is jockeying to the baddest struggle bottom on the block. Sexually, that's a good a look. Bottoms make the world go 'round, but in the struggle, it reifies the power of the system or entity doing the fucking, or perhaps raping. Smile if you want, but this ain't sex, you ain't give consent, and putting a smile on a struggle doesn't give you any more power.

Which brings us back to the topic at hand, why work "hard"–or do anything hard–if you don't have to? What is the necessity of struggle? What is the value of obstacles? Don't we deserve for things to come easily, naturally and without a pound of flesh or stress? Why is it that we value the artist who declines our offer because s/he is double booked, more than we value the sister that readily accepts our offer? Why do we value the person who rarely responds to our messages on time—conjuring anxieties around self-worth, value and beauty—more than we value the one who readily gives their space, time and love, affirming our essence? Why do we value the job opportunity that put us through weeks of hellish interviews more than the one that hired us on the spot? All too often we find our worth, and those of our "loved" ones in the practices of devaluation and the politics of accessibility.

This is true in the work that we do to earn our wages but also in the practice of love. All too often I've been a willing participant in the perversion of the practice of love. The notion that love, like life, must indeed require hard work. Those things that come easily must be studiously avoided or surveilled with a watchful eye, yours and that of the community. Those men that have loved me immediately, I held at bay, thinking they must have been crazy to get involved so quickly. They were too accessible. Clearly they did not value themselves or, alternatively, their personal equity was coasting quite close to E. Those that are readily accessible are valued less than those that are hard to get, hard to text, rare to return calls, mysterious. This is nothing short of a personal and communal ideology of intimate capitalisms.

"*Maybe I liked the stress, cuz I was*

young restless. But that was

long ago, I don't wanna

cry no'mo."

-Mary J. Blige, No More Drama

The gag here, is that the emotionally impoverished are the most circumspect about love that comes easy. We reject love that comes easily because, secretly, we do not value ourselves enough to see that we are worthy. We think we must perform acrobatics, break down walls, perform some herculean feat in order to prove worthy of loving. We must learn that access giving freely is not a statement of unworthiness, but a demonstration of wholehearted living. We must nurture a belief and knowledge that whether this love, this opportunity, this space works out or not, we shall leave whole and with all the worth that we came in with. All too often we limit our practice of love to capitalist models. We diminish ourselves in thinking that our love, our essence, our greatness is a finite resource—as well as our ability to participate in such unions or experiences—thereby shrinking our divine nature into capitalistic, fickle models of the mass production of love. The fact is, love cannot be mass produced and neither is it finite.

Palestine

Blackness, Palestine & Solidarity: A Call for A Critical Love Ethic

This piece was originally published in the Tufts Daily in March, 2013.

The story of the African Diaspora's journey from the bondages of the Atlantic to the post-racialist age of Obama is a topic of critical discussion in many anti-racist communities, a point of pride for neo-liberal allies and a rallying cry for those currently pondering the efficacy of race-based remedies for problems based in historical (and present) white supremacist policies. For me and many of my African-American peers, our history functions on an axis. It is simultaneously a painful pressure point and a source of unspeakable pride and joy. Our histories of oppressions and strategic survival bind us together like the hermetic locks of our Ashanti, Maasai, Yoruba and Mau Mau ancestors. Each day as we live and breathe we carry with us the revolutionary rage of Nat Turner and Angela Davis, the intellectual prowess of Dubois, Douglass and Kimberlé Crenshaw, the strategic acuity of Tubman and Malcolm and the empowering love ethics of Ella Baker, Fannie Lou and bell hooks. The lesson of our histories is one of community, love, resistance and radical solidarity.

The quest for Black liberation in the United States was aided by white allies, Jewish-Americans in particular. Thurgood Marshall, the first black Supreme Court Justice and lead litigator in Brown v. Board of Education, routinely recalled the assistance and support he received from his middle-class Jewish neighbors. The history of Black Americans and Jewish Americans is storied, well documented and an important part of the Civil Rights Movement. Many young Jewish college students participated in the freedom rides down South to participate in sit-ins, marches and other demonstrations. Jewish youth routinely put their bodies and privilege on the line to stand in solidarity against the interconnected systems of racism, classism, nativism, anti-Semitism, fundamental anti-blackness and white supremacy that defined the Black and Jewish experiences in America. As a young Black male who benefited greatly from the coalitions before and during the Civil Rights Movement, I would be remiss without recounting the ways in which our Jewish brothers and sisters have assisted in our historic, shared fights for liberation and human dignity.

Just as the relationship between Jewish Americans and African Americans was based in a fundamental understanding and experience of racial and ethnic subordination, so too is the relationship between the African and Palestinian diasporas. Our lives are similarly defined, redefined and experienced through the systemic maldistribution of material resources and inequitable access to sociopolitical power(s). Our ancestors have both experienced the traumas of violent, forced immigration from lands we have historically called home. Palestinians continue to exist through deep resistance in what Angela Davis has called the "largest open-air prison" in the world. They are policed, profiled and subordinated

186

through terroristic, violent lessons of racialized comportment. According to Alice Walker, "Going through Israeli checkpoints is like going back in time to [the] American Civil Rights struggle." As a Black man, in the present age, I will never understand the physical and psychological traumas of a Palestinian brother at an Israeli checkpoint. However, my experiences with police and racial profiling and the real threat of being assassinated for walking while black, or wearing a hoodie, or appearing too aggressive allow me to retain a deep empathy for his experience. As I mourn the murders of Trayvon Martin and Jordan Davis, I must also grieve for the lives Samir Ahmad Abdul-Rahim and Mohammed Salayme. For too many young men and women of color, survival itself is a revolutionary act of resistance.

To be born Palestinian is to be legally marked as inherently violent, indisputably dangerous and a necessary gudgeon for the peace and calm of "civilized" society. Put simply, the Palestinian body has been constructed as the threat to Israeli society, creating a state of vast acceptance and normalization of the current state-sanctioned system of racial apartheid that has displaced millions of Palestinian bodies. Just as nearly 600,000 Black and Latino young men are routinely harassed by police under the pretenses of New York City's "stop and frisk" policy, millions of Palestinian people are terrorized for drifting too far from the walls of an open-air prison. In both cases, data shows that the "threat" is rarely material but, instead, psychological. These systems of racial "othering" continually create imputed images of people of color as inherently threatening and dangerous. This internal logic equates Black and Palestinian existences. This logic paves the way for violent and strictly enforced racist policies. In short, these policies enhance, benefit and reify the power and humanity of one racial group at the expense of the other.

Let me be clear, however, my criticism is not one of hate or malice toward individual Israelis but instead a critical analysis of the powers and effects of settler colonialism, racial subordination, Zionism and controlling images that allow such bloodshed to continue unabated. The issue here is not the rational fear of the Israeli man or woman who recalls the horrors of their history, but instead the ways in which state policies have perpetuated racial subordination and violent trauma through the molestation of the bloody chronicle of Jewish death and survival, all in the name of peace and safety. We cannot protect ourselves, our essence, or our humanity from systemic violence with systemic violence. Instead, we must adopt a critical love ethic of universal liberation from cyclical and systemic violence and oppression.

We are called to remember that our willful participation in such systems, regardless of our intentions, taints the humanity that our ancestors lived and died to achieve. It has been said that "the master's tools will never dismantle the master's house." This is indeed true, because it is through the utilization of the tools of oppression that we become both the (material) oppressor and the (spiritually) oppressed. In order to move past these cyclical patterns of violence and trauma we must look deeply and examine the oppressor within, dare to love those who we see as threats or "other" and question whether the threat is real, imagined or internal. This is a call for a human solidarity across and beyond racial differences and an ethic of love that first acknowledges our shared humanity and endeavors to reify that shared notion. Distinct from mere alliance, solidarity calls for a recognition and dismembering of the systems that throughout time have crushed us all by guaranteeing the safety of some at the cost of death for others. Solidarity recognizes that our humanity and survival are eternally linked with the dignity and lives of those deemed least among. Without solidarity there can be no love and without love there can be no peace or justice. For these reasons I stand with love and solidarity with the people of Palestine and all those whose lives and humanity have been and continue to be destroyed, distorted or denied.

7/16/14

4PM

In Remembrance of The Children

Mohammad, 9

Mohammad, 11

Ahed, 10

and

Zakaria Baker, 10.

These cousins, these children, aged 9-11, were killed by Israeli bombs in their family's fisherman shack, just off the beach at 4pm. Don't tell me this is about Hamas when 80% of the slain are civilians. Death is the consequence of global apathy, indifference and complicity.

Brothers, you are not forgotten.

Midnight Thoughts On Children in Palestine, Authorized Death & Other Approved Violence

I was reading a piece—from a place I can't recall—with a quotation that pierced my soul. The phrase stated "I've learned that – and this is just one example of many – a Palestinian child has tragically been killed every three days for the past 14 years. That bears repeating, since such deaths are rarely, if ever, given any attention in America: Palestinian parents have had to bury a child every three days for the past 14 years." I already knew that but here I sit.

I sat there, on my couch, drinking Merlot and watching an HBO special on Public Defenders in the deep, American south. I reread the quote over and over. I thought of my friends that reside in Palestine, Sami, Tamara and many more—as well as those whose families were displaced long before their birth. In a classic act of selfishness, I began to ponder what my life would be like if there were no Sami? Who would challenge me to speak my truths, my multiple (compounded) existences as BlaQueer and poor? How would I have found my voice? Would I have known the podium to be a place of freedom and terror-demolition? Would I know my gift—my self–that I was indeed exceedingly excellent by virtue of my survival? Then what of Tamara? How would I have learned the importance of art to humanistic existence and resistance? Would I have known existence as a form of resistance? What of the love she gave me through my ill-fated relationship, the tears she caught from my cheek and the love she pumped into my heart? Then I left Narciss where he belonged–far from this conversation–and began to think about bodies, Palestinian bodies. Bodies born to die.

What can be said to a child who knows death as the most consistent part of their living? No, not death by natural causes but violent, intentional, maiming death of bodies, spirits, hopes, communities and nations? I say death, as opposed to murder, because murder is more kind and is done by seemingly controllable human beings on a small scale. However, death is uncontrollable. There seem to be few deterrents. It is knows no law, no God and no love for humanity. Death lays in wait in the bones to attack the heart who dares to grasp hope. Death does not care, because it doesn't see–or allow one to realize–humanity. What do we say to the child? How can one go play in the streets, when the sidewalk seems to concocting a plan with death and may ex/implode at any time? How shall we cajole a young lady to go to school, when death and the walls of the school house might indeed crush them beneath their collective weight? Can we tell a child to drink their 64oz of water, when death and the water have mated, and 95% of Gaza's water is unfit to wet their whistle into living? What do we say to the children of Palestine, besides what they already know: They are not children of the world, but chattel of Death…and Israel.

Many lives have been stolen in Palestine–boys, girls, women and men–and many have been killed in Israel. I'm not quite sure what to do about this, but I will continue to stress and present the humanity of all

Palestinians, because their humanity does not seem to be a commonly held fact. We must see the linkages between our humanity and the dehumanization of all other living–and stolen–peoples, lest we continue to lose our grasp on reality and the pulse of our hearts. I hope that I will soon have the opportunity to give my talents to this community of Warrior-Survivors, to aid in their journey toward and freedom and our collective redemption as humans with bloodstained hands.

LETTERS OF LOVE, HOME, & OTHER IMAGINATIVES

Brother to Brother: Hari & Me

Kindling A Fire That Heals

A series of letters, exchanges of love and healings, from BlaQueer brothers across space, and often violent, times.

My Brother Hari,

There is so much on my mind, but in the midst of it all, I somehow find myself reaching back to you, back to home. As I sit to write, I'm positioned in a magnificent place of privilege. It's astounding. I'm here in Cape Town, taking law classes at the University of Western Cape, through my home school, Howard University School of Law. I'm currently zoning in and out of my comparative criminal law course but I'm guilty of the same behavior in my comparative constitutional law course. Statutes of limitations, Oscar Pistoria, human dignity, the richest man in China, FIFA, Bashir and Mother Emmanuel. Mother Emmanuel.

That is where my ears perk up. It heartens me to see my frumpy, white law professor–a former federal prosecutor–going on and on about this case, with great passion. He speaks with authority–after all, prosecuting this shit was his job. But his passion, though refreshing, is suffocating. We are speaking about legalese, not lives. He speaks about the complicated nature of the flag, not the straight forward representation of racial-sexual terrors. My peers, listen and zone out. Black, African-American, white and colored. They have colored folks here–essentially light skin niggas that are deemed too good (read: white) to be black. Being colored isn't necessarily a biological condition–both parents can be black and you can be colored if you're light–white-ish–enough. It's a sociopolitical designation, with cultural, economic, social and psychological consequences. None of them get it, none of my peers. They want their degrees. They don't have time to feel..or perhaps that don't remember how to feel? I wonder if the mechanisms of their mind and body have been so mauled the white supremacist, heteropatriachal, capitalistic society that they have been dis-membered and the process of re-membering is too violent, too distant, too impossible to mesh with necessity of their callous survival? Perhaps it's by choice. Perhaps they don't give a fuck. Perhaps they're just "New Blacks." But the only difference between "New Blacks" and other blacks is a bow tie, pressed shirt and relationship to a capitalistic hustle. One group refuses to pimp out their souls..and those their kin. I don't know what they are, but I know they are different and I know they know.

It's interesting here, for me, to be in a seat of educational privilege–psychological warfare–while simultaneously unable to use such privilege/proximity to affect the realities of black genocide. If the role of the white supremacy is to "distract" as Mother Toni states, it has succeeded in this moment. This suspension, in a state of immobility and helplessness, has rendered me emotionally exhausted and intellectually paralyzed. I often ponder the value of my intellect, if it is unable to translate to liberation of some type. This trap; the notion that our value as BlaQueer, black and oppressed peoples is intimately tied to our ability to create and produce

196

liberations, critical love ethics/practices and survival practices..is the most effective and dominant narrative of (internalized) white supremacies among the black learned class. Consider the consequences…the most learned and talented and/or creative among us–fuck the traditional measuring of excellence by society btw—are being consumed by internal embers of unworthiness, self loathing and rage..for our inability to break every chain…effectively tying a noose around our necks, in the name of the people, our people…who are wondering wtf is wrong with our angry yet unbothered, loving yet callous, hopeful yet pessimistic asses.

I sit here in Africa, South Africa, at the edges of the continent realizing that though I am here..and surely some of my people came from this continent..I can never truly be here. As the sun touches my flesh on the beaches of Cape Town, my thoughts slowly carry across the Atlantic, as I think about my brothers being consumed, maligned, maimed and slain under the same sun. I wonder if it was hot on their flesh, causing trickles of sweat down strong, running backs, yearning for escape and survival. Or perhaps, the sun was comforting on the east side of Oakland, as two BlaQueer fathers walk their daughter to the park, to teach her how fly a kite..while learning themselves the value and importance of pure love through eyes and unrelenting affection and dedication to them, despite their flaws and because of their subversive, familial love? But I always return to the guilt of travel, survival, distance from death….the failure of not writing with enough flair or fire to save our lives…or sipping a latte and having a champion-bred poodle…when a black mother is struggling to get WIC…we can call this the black savior complex…or survivors guilt..perhaps its contrived..or perhaps it's real? What are willing or required to do for our liberation as individuals and collective? Is there a real collective? I don't know, love, but in writing to you..I hope to demonstrate a willingness to build and open up a dialogue beyond just us, about the cost, benefits, problems and promises of a new critical love ethic and practices of love.

How are you? How is your writing? I know you've been aching. I wish I could ache and pain. But I'm floating…suspended somewhere in a unfeeling, exhausted state of disbelief and unknowing. I've been unable to compose essays…so poetry has documented my life and fleeting thoughts. I look forward to hearing your voice through the text.

In a Boundless Love,

-T

Tabias,

It's so great to read your words. I think a more accurate description would be that it's great to feel them. To feel your spirit and know that I am not alone.

In addition to pain and grief, but also in addition to the joy and inspiration I've received from watching you and other brothers and sisters who have responded to the events in Charleston in ways that refill the reserve of strength I was nearly sure I'd lost forever, I've been feeling an overwhelming sense of loneliness since those 9 lives were stolen from Mother Emmanuel. I feel now, more than ever, that I fit neither here nor there – in neither Black spaces nor white spaces nor any other People of Color spaces – in neither men spaces nor women spaces nor gender non-conforming spaces – in neither queer spaces nor straight spaces. I do not fit in my family.

I have struggled with loneliness a lot. As a fellow Black queer man in an anti-Black, anti-queer world, I'm sure you know this feeling, too. But I have never been so seized by this fear that if I reached the end of my rope and I didn't have my home or a stable mind there would be no other spaces for me to go. No other spaces that are, at least mostly, safe. I do not know where these spaces exist anymore nor if they even do. I feel safe now, though. Writing this. Reading your letter. Maybe this is one of those spaces.

Two days ago, I fought using the last bit of strength my spirit could muster to get my older brother to understand me and my love for Black and Brown communities and how it is not anti-white-people. It was a traumatizing conversation, as I thought that in my family was the last place my love for anyone would be questioned. I should have known better, though. I keep pretending as if I'm not the only queer child in the family or not the one who rarely gets a phone call or the one least interested in many of the things they are interested in. I thought that none of that should matter when it comes to questions of love, though, but it does and always has. They mattered when I came out and, though they defended me, my siblings insisted I "try to understand" when my parents refused to no longer pay for my education because of it. I wonder, have any of them tried to understand that I don't think there's anything in that decision that warrants understanding? They mattered when they contended, despite my protests, that they could understand my queerness just as well as I could. I wonder, do they understand that I don't even understand my queerness as much as I just live it? They mattered when this same brother's friend said he liked our family because we weren't like other Black people and they said my anger in response was wrong. I wonder, why is it always the response to wrong that is wrong with them?

You ask if I even believe there is a collective. I wonder…

Does a family have to be safe to be a family? Mine is not. I love my family more than anyone else, but I am not safe with them. Why does it always feel like me against a collective, when they are my family just like they are each other's?

So my being different matters in questions of love.

I feel safe reading how sometimes you feel like your peers just don't get it because sometimes I feel that way too. Even the Black ones. The concept of colored that you have there is foreign to me, but if they aren't that here, they're "New Black". If they're not "New Black", they're anti-queer; if they're not anti-queer, they're misogynoiristic; and on and on down the rabbit hole. And sometimes it feels like I hate them for that. And I think that's one of the most powerful functions of white supremacy – it turns privilege within a marginalized group into a special kind of privilege that does a special kind of damage. It allows cishet Black men to physically and emotionally violate Black women and queer and trans Black men more than anyone else without cishet white men getting their hands dirty. It allows me to feel like I hate my brothers for this.

It allows me to lash out at my family.

And maybe that works on an internal level too. Maybe intellectual privilege consumes us so – exhausts us so – because it is too a special kind of privilege and does a special kind of damage. Maybe this damage is best described as an inability to love and trust in a healthy way.

Maybe my brother was right to question my love.

Maybe I question the idea of a collective and we question our-
selves and he questioned me and I question my family because we have
been let down so many times that we are forgetting how to love and trust.
And I'm forgetting how to rest because I don't trust the world not to
crumble if I do. And if the world crumbles it will be my fault because:
Black savior complex.

But the world has been crumbling around Black and Brown com-
munities for several centuries and I haven't been around for most of those
centuries to deserve the blame. Maybe it has stopped already and we just
haven't cleaned up the destructive mess left behind. You ask, "What are
we willing or required to do for our liberation as individuals and a collec-
tive?" Maybe it has something to do with that – cleaning up this mess.
And no, I don't mean that in the bullshit way people imply when they say
we have to focus on fixing our communities first before addressing white
racism. I mean that maybe we have to learn how to better love each other
through the mess? Maybe we have to re-learn how to love ourselves
through it? Maybe the abuses our brothers and sisters rain down on us
matter in questions of love, matter in how we express it to them, but we
must resist questioning the love we have for them and ourselves? And love
doesn't mean not fighting. The opposite, actually. If I love you – really
love you – I would lay down my life for you. And lay down my life to stop
you from hurting the rest of us.

I don't know what this all looks like. I've tried to define it before,
but I don't know if I was comprehensive. Maybe we need to define it bet-

ter. What do you think? How would you start defining what a love for one another and ourselves through the crumbled mess that makes us hurt each other should look like?

I'm jealous of you. I need a break from this place, too. But breaks are a mirage because I know there are no breaks regardless of how far you go to escape, and I think you know it too – that's why you keep finding yourself reaching back to home. So for now I'll find safety in these words. Write back soon.

With love,

HZ

This the third segment of a four part series, between myself and Hari Ziyad of RaceBaitr. After witnessing weeks of violence birthed from white supremacies, coupled with bursts of queer victories, we decided to create a healing space together where could process the intersections of our Black & Queer existences. We invite you to join us. To catch up on the dialogue, read the original post here and his response–which this is referring to–here.

Hari,

I hold you in my heart, from here. With each line of your prose, I find myself, holding myself, because I too feel safe(r) and you're too far to feel the strength of my grasp. I find peace here, with you. With you knowing me..and us knowing each other..privately..publicly. There is something to the public displaying of black love, black brotherhood. It doesn't happen often. It's often messy, confusing and bubbly over with things we'd rather not discuss–usually things that must be discussed for home and healing. Perhaps through this, we'll put one foot forward in the practice of loving blackness, BlaQueerness and creating holistic relationships and practices of relating.

Feeling is something isn't? Those internal stirrings seem to always govern our external doings, despite our constant professions of "not being in our feelings." The truth seems to be closer to the fact that we are our feelings, beneath and through the masks, our true selves are quite ungovernable. Perhaps this is the violence of the collective. In our yearnings to create, identify and heal and "our" we often sacrifice many of those

204

perfect imperfections of "i" and "you." We fear, or more accurately, I often feel myself practicing that horrid tradition of internal, cultural and political circumcision to create a space of "home" in/through/with the collective… all while failing to realize that the scalpel, is of course, the most sophisticated of the master's tools..and those tools have but one purpose..to maintain the power of the plantation and the immobility of those daring enough to be sharecroppers, seeking a modicum of independence.

That feeling of loneliness. He is such a daddyfucker. He used to come to me in the evenings, uninvited, sullying my once joyful dreams. It came to the point where I had so dreaded evenings, darkness, that I'd read and write and run myself into exhaustion as to prevent my mind being able to conjure up anymore thoughts or dreams attached to loneliness. That worked for a time, but a short time. Through the writings of Essex, Joseph, Audre and bell, I came to fear and understand that loneliness is truly a side-effect of home. No, not the home we've been speaking of consisting of loved and dreaded ones, but home within. All too often I believe, we especially, confuse houses with homes. We concern ourselves with the happenings of folks, the thoughts of folks, the fears and fuckery of folks that we are only temporally, contractually and tentatively bound to. I've never been a fan of being bound. But home, for me, is a place within. A place where I reside with all of me. It is a warm, cozy and safe place. It where my fears meet my truths and my truths converse with my hopes and they with my insecurities all together with the promise and fact of who I am, who i'm being called to be and the annoyingly, small, high pitched chants of those trying to walk away with all my stuff. In my home, I've been allowed to create, remodel and own a space where I am forever a lone, but never longing. Intimate knowledge and love of oneself creates a prescient sense of awareness that other cannot understand. This sort of self love, and it's attending practices, creates a sort of insulation and distancing from what much of our loved ones and society see as normal..the chase to fit in, smile at all costs and be pleasant and desired. When you at home, you don't have to cover yourself with clothes, you can choose to be naked, and smile.

I tried to speak of love here, when thinking about the black connection to a free Palestine. A sort of thinking through the notion of a "critical love ethic."

You spoke of understanding. Perhaps understanding isn't what we should be fighting or longing for? As you noted, we often don't understand ourselves. Centering love, and by extension humanization, on understanding positions the othered sister/brother in the realm of the sleepless educator..who must know the world, know the student and know thyself. Our bodies can no longer be chalkboards, emblazoned and engraved with bloody tales of trauma, overcoming and lessons on how not to be an

emotional terrorists. Like you said brother, perhaps it's just about living. So many of us are stuck in survival, we have forgotten, or never had the chance, to experience the freedom of simply living. We are often so caught up with white supremacist, capitalistic, heteropatriarchal, trans*phobic society that we forget the centrality of the beating heart, the thinking mind and spirits that know truths deeper than Euphrates and longer than the Nile.

The Black Savior Complex is so unique. It posits the dual question and mandate If I don't save me, and us, who will? If I fail, then I have reified white supremacies and midwifed black deaths. As brave as it may sound, there are far too many casualties in these ideologies of heroism, mainly the heroine.

I am rambling now, as a protective exercise. Really, I wanted to speak with you about yesterday. We texted briefly about this. Shockingly, or unsurprisingly perhaps, I'm finding it hard to express what I intimated or at least hinted at over text, through this public space. So I'll try. The Slave Lodge almost killed me. The Slave Lodge almost killed me. The Slave Lodge almost killed me.

Breathe. As I was texting you, I had simply needed a breathe. I needed to remember that the slave deck I had just laid myself on was not a threat, no longer. I needed to know that the chains and ropes I had laid over my body, to re-member ourstories, were not knotted. I had to reach out to you, just to know that I could Hari. A heaviness had overcome me as I read and chanted the over two hundred names scrawled on that wheel of remembrance. I had taken the chains and ropes off my body, but they had never really left. Our mothers bore the physical weight deprivation of these tools of genocide, yet we continued to be choked and slowly euthanized by them today. The ropes have become guns, the ships white supremacist nations where physical escape is tantamount to jumping into an ocean and praying for a miracle…only to realize that you can only be found by another Savior, and to her, you're still just another, other. I couldn't't breathe. I still can't breathe. We are no longer slaves. We are not enslaved people. In some ways, it feels like we are worse…partly because we dwell, celebrate and elope in the mess you spoke of earlier…adorning ourselves with its stink…perhaps because within we know there is no escaping–not in this life–and better to survive with the pretense of autonomy, than to die, throat-chopped by reality and rejection, chasing liberation.

To think of these things here has been quite difficult. I'll write more about this later. I just had to share this last bit with you. They feed off of my African-Americanness. All of them. Even within Africa, South Africa, MY blackness is a property I have no title over. If I am to be owned, again, I had hoped to be all mine. The black and colored South Africans position themselves as friendly and close only after they here of my American accent. Otherwise I'm invisible, or a pest, to be watched. They are white supremacists too. However, it isn't my passport they seem to crave. No, it is the erotic of the African-American mystique…the Nigga in me..they can't get enough of that word. When it is spoken to me, here, by them.."neeee-guhh" it sends a strange sense of strangulation, anger and envy through my body. Strangled, because I have no words they care to understand or receive. Angry because even in the Motherland, my body and reality is positioned as cultural or economic capital…everyone wants to be a nigga until the struggle is real. Envious..because to be black, to be a real nigga, without a white state, mass white violence/anxieties, the fear of the police's gun…incongruent echoes of Malcolm, Assata, Martin, Angela..cultural voyeurism, the raping of African-American struggle and brilliance is violent..and surviving is fucking up my BlaQueerflow. I can breathe again, but I have only so many smiles left.

Looking forward to your words. They take me back to the moment we met. The sun was warm and shining, the shisha was strong and brotherhood was brewing.

In Liberatory Love,

Tabias

Tabias,

I have stopped and started this letter over and over for days now. I keep finding myself writing my thoughts down for just a few moments before erasing them. Breathing. Thinking. Writing again. Erasing. Breathing. Thinking. Refusing to feel. There's so much to feel right now. It's as though my skin has been rubbed off and every speck of dust in every gust of wind creates a new abrasion. So I've been wrapped away, unable to write to you because my words were packed behind this covering I've put on to keep the dirt from my raw skin.

But, yes, feeling is something. Maybe feeling is everything. Today, I feel good again. No, not happy. I haven't been happy since Charleston, but good. Uncovering myself and letting myself feel loneliness, sorrow, pain, anger and grief has been freeing. The dust doesn't sting anymore. You'd have never guessed, but it actually seems to be creating a new layer of protection! These are human feelings. They exist for a reason. Who said they have no purpose? Why do we try so hard to suffocate them? They are a part of me. Not just sadness, no, but not just happiness either. All of them.

It's so funny that you mention it because I've been thinking quite a bit about the master's house and Audre Lorde's quote on how the master's tools will never dismantle it. I don't think tools always have to be used according to their design, though. Let me tell you a story: yesterday, I found myself finally putting together the shelf I bought for my room. I

210

needed to drill holes to affix it to my wall, but I didn't have the right drill bit. I used a larger bit that I had lying around to create an indent big enough to rest the screw so that it could make its own hole. These are the kinds of things you learn when your father insists that men know how to use tools, and you hate him for it.

My point is, the scalpel may be designed to maintain the order of the plantation, but maybe you can also use it to cut the wires that power the lights so that you can make your escape? Maybe we too often forget the next part of Lorde's quote, "They may allow us to temporarily beat him at his own game?"

Maybe, sometimes, that temporary relief is just what we need?

I see now that I never valued that inner home that you describe. I knew it was there, but I did not like being alone and I didn't know how to let others in, so I was forever away from it. It's still unfurnished, cold and bare. I had abandoned it, covering my skin from whatever was in the wind, using that scalpel the way it was designed: for this bloody cultural and political circumcision, severing parts of me to be with a collective.

I know now I need this home. I know it is, at the very least, safe. I know it houses all of me and all of my emotions and I know that each of them play an integral role in my life. I know no one will ever live here with me.

I want visitors, though. While I'm buying furniture and finding comfort and making this neglected place livable, I'm also pulling the shades and opening the blinds. I'm unlocking the door and playing in the yard. I want you over for wine and hookah. Not every day. Not everyone. But some days. Someone. People like you.

No one will ever know all of my secret nooks and crannies. No one will know exactly who I am and what I am feeling. I'm still discovering new rooms and windows myself, and I certainly need to spend more time doing that, but I can't stay here alone all the time.

I think building a community and maintaining one's home are not mutually exclusive. And yet, I cannot seem to find a balance. I am traumatized by my family, friends and loved ones, or I am wallowing in loneliness. I am trying to understand others, but spending no time understanding myself. I am welcoming someone into my circle, and they stab me in the back. I am choosing to survive and forgetting to live. I am choosing to live and forgetting to survive.

I have to be both/and and not either/or – I know that now. I need to survive AND live. I have to allow myself to feel joy AND despair. I must respond to loneliness AND overcrowding. Have my home AND my guests. That's easier said than done, I know, but I'm tired of complaining about the fucking tight rope and ready to learn how to walk it. Will you train with me?

I'm sorry I could not respond more consistently while you were at The Slave Lodge. My skin was still raw then. I could not think about the millions who died before us and those who are constantly dying today at the same time. I am bombarded with Black death. It's there and it's real, but so is Black joy. So is the amazing weekend we spent together in DC. So is that Black baby's smile I saw today in the arms of his father; the man who wasn't supposed to be holding him, because Black fathers are constructed as chronically, inherently absent. We can have both. I should have responded. Black death does not mean Black lives don't exist. Black joy does not have to mean the Black struggle isn't real.

And your smile is not a finite resource. I'll make sure of that.

Going to buy this tightrope now – I hope to hear from you very soon.

With much love,

Hari

To The Children Who Come Next
Eli, Emani & Davieyon

My Beloveds,

I write to you from a place both far and near. I've watched you grow in the heartland while living in cities from coast to coast and contending with the great in-betweens of living here and there, while black, coming from where we are from. Despite my reticence, your beauty is a constant reminder of the importance of family, the endurance of hope and the necessity of the love-labor I profess and hope to accomplish throughout my lifetime. Home is dangerous place. Home is often where the hatred is. I trust that you have not learned this yet your mother and father, my siblings, know the price of such a blood-stained gift. We learned early on the practice of self-hate, gleaned from ill-informed lessons of survival, strength and fluidity. To be clear, we were never hated by anyone within our family: people lived and died for our chances to be. However, sometimes that "be" and that sacrifice had unintended consequences. You see, working backbreaking hours to care for a child, a grandchild, cousin or even your younger siblings has a cost. What one sees as love—say providing meals and stability—may be experienced as pain or even hate, if it is accompanied with a scowl and has insufficient energy or faculty to profess and articulate such loving kindness. Do not trouble your spirits if your mother or father fails to reflexively smile when they look upon your face. The struggle of being a working black mother or father forces one to ration what outward joy s/he has left. Survival jujitsu is an expensive practice that takes more than it gives. You see, your mother wakens in the morning to see that you have joy throughout the day. Your father's heart smiles when hears your name, it reminds him that life has meaning, has power and that hope is not something stolen so easily. When they go into the world, before you, making room for you, their smiles and laughter are often stolen by people—and their toxic ways of living—that will see never you, or anyone else, as human. This psychosis is not your concern. You see, some folks consume blackness as elixir for the inadequacies and anxieties of their broken spirits. Your parents go forth and clear the way so that you might not have to encounter such parasitic peoples. You are loved, you are a source of joy, you are the hope of our family circle and none of us will have your soul disrupted by the ill and ill-intentioned. But you must'n blame my siblings, your parents, for they are engaged in a battle for your continued freedom, for your liberation. Where their lips do not part, or when their voices are raised, know that their spirit powers their body, daily, from the wells of their love and hopes for you.

You are young, but I want you to know this. Love is not simply about how much of your body you are willing, able or compelled to destroy or trade in for wealth accumulation in the name of stability. To be sure, these are hearty sacrifices. But love, love is much more expensive—though it may often include the example given above—it is a practice. Love is an investment un-reliant upon personal enrichment. It is not capitalistic. It is an investment in individual, mutual and interconnected humanity. It is the mutual, individual and co-investment in the lover and beloveds individual, collective and communal growth. This growth encompasses the emotional, intellectual, spiritual, economic and cosmic realms. It is a recognition of the interconnected nature of our humanity and the permission to simply be, you, always. It is a promise and commitment to free you from the costs of one's insecurities and the societal and state-mandated consequences freedom. This is love. We all know this, yet, we are afraid to speak its name and midwife its existences, beloved. Because to speak of it, is a sore reminder of its absence and too often, to practice it, is to risk the pain of its revocation. Better then, some elders reckon, to leave love and good enough alone. Children born free cannot accept such folly, you cannot afford it. Learn love for yourself. Walk into love, read and share your truths as much as possible: then you will become familiar with yourself, comfortable with vulnerability and free to be who you are, wherever you are. Always, always, tell yourself the truth, even when you don't want to hear it. Despite its mosquito-like persona, the truth does nothing but heal and re-center our values, no matter how jarring its entry.

In your minds, perhaps even your hearts, I imagine that I remain a small part of your imagination: that uncle often spoken of but rarely seen, apart from a random, unannounced hours long visit from some foreign place you may have never heard of. You are right, I have long been worlds away, but my mind, heart and spirit have never left you. Please know that I've been with you from the moment your parents, my siblings, first opined about your possible existence. I was there, making way, calming nerves, sending love and hoping to be an uncle that was more useful than violent, more loving than mysterious and more consistent than domineering. I could not bear to be near you when my own illness—that of imputed anxieties, identities and problematic practices—were alive and highly contagious. I had to demonstrate to myself that I was indeed *my self.* This is no small feat and it is an ongoing process. I have had to—and continue to —learn things about myself that must be unlearned. Each day I realize that there some piece of me that remains circumcised, forged from my soul at the threshing floor of social cues, that has yet to be re-membered. To become whole again, to become free, requires and unbecoming of all the badges and incidences of the process of becoming black, of becoming gendered, of becoming classed, of becoming first in the line of inheritance of cisheteropatriarchy, sexism, misogyny, ableism, nativism, racial ideologies and capitalist orientations. I'm still learning how to love people, to love me and to be both queer and liminal. You see, I cannot fathom being a parasite that feeds on the humanity of others—in the production of the dehumanized—in order to *feel* secure and free myself. Race, gender, sexuality, class, sex, nationhood: none of these things are real. They are tacit, agreements meant to keep the American Daydream intact—while obscuring the reality, the lived effects of the American Nightmare—that we hew too, because it offers all of us something unique, distinct and perhaps some situational privilege in comparison to the next categorized body.

Talking Back, Talking Black, Hearing Me
5, 15, 25

Oh Honey 5,

Those full cheeks and beautiful, brown eyes show both the youthfulness of your flesh and the age of your spirit. You are no one's accident and it is ok to cry. Even your name speaks of the great purpose and importance you hold. Tabias: The goodness, greatness or blessings of God and Olajuawon: wealth and honor are God's gift. You hold many secrets, far too many for a child, but you wear them well. I promise you though, shug, they'll only weigh you down. Secrets don't protect you, but wall you off from the most crucial pieces of yourself. Don't spend too much time worrying about dying, you've got at least 21 more years to live. Some terrible things have and will happen to you, but don't put down your pen. It is mighty heavy to lift, once it has fallen, and it is your most powerful tool besides that voice of yours. Yes, yes, you've realized you are a black but don't be traumatized. I know you felt different, jumping in the pool, the only black boy there and all alone? But loneliness isn't what struck you, it was the hair. Aaron's thick, golden locs laid flat when he emerged from the water and you'd never seen anything quite like it. You wonder why your hair doesn't lay down? You wonder if something is wrong with your scalp? And why did your skin turn all white? Well baby, that is just a matter of Black Folks Magic! Yes, darling! Most things in this world are controlled by the cosmic rules of gravity. It holds things down to the ground,

218

lest they fly away and are lost to the universe. But your hair is special! It's magic! It defies gravity and stands strong and thick and dark and tall no matter the circumstances! Water, rain, snow, sunshine: the power of your locs know no season or reason to bow before any man, woman, child or circumstance. If you look closely, your hair is teaching you a lesson: never compromise yourself, shrink your height or bow in anyone's presence. Be the mystifying person—gravity defying soul—that you were meant to be! And your skin? Just as your hair won't fall, neither will your skin burn on the hottest suns. They call you black but you come from the light, don't be afraid to light up a room, a heart or tragic darkness when time is right, Son of Olorun.

I mustn't keep you from playing but I want to address the issue of maleness. You've seen some things that you can't shake from your mind. Nightmares of violent men—you've yet to meet a peaceful one—hurting children, hurting momma, hurting grandma, hurting you. I remember too. I was there. I still hear the screaming and that quieting moment when her head came through the window with Bill's long, outstretched fingers wrapped around her neck and eyes that saw you and saw through you. He was promising to kill her. You thought you were dead. You could only think about that single drop of blood falling—perhaps attempting to escape, you thought—through the center of your cotton candy. You wondered if you were dead yet. But you weren't, so you ran, letting your bladder free as you did. You didn't care, you saw a man, and you needed your grandmother, lest you become a man too. I remember you admonishing your "thing" to fall off. You loved it, it was yours, you just didn't want to hit your momma, or grandma or cousins or anyone..but that was just what men did. You were gearing up for your first circumcision, because it was better to let that "man" thing go than to lose or harm those that loved you. Oh beloved! Those were scary times and men are often scary folks but this need not be your destiny. You were born with your body and you are its master. You need not be violent, evil or unforgiving. You just need to be you. The man you saw, is not the person you are. Always, always, always, think of yourself as Tabias first and foremost. Let the men take care of themselves.

Beloved 15,

I see you, drenched in the tears of the prayerful and homeless. You belong, perhaps not where you are, perhaps not to the church or the circumstances of your birth, but you belong to you. There is no shame in tears, do not fret. They are simply a reminder that while you are not yet home. They are a reminder to build, but first you must be aware of the tools, materials and desires that you harbor. You are the architect of this life, the carpenter, the construction worker, the interior designer and of course, the owner. It is high time you know that you are in control and you are the only one who can truly value or devalue that beautiful soul.

I saw you before, sitting on the sofa, with more tears. You had that knife, the one Neil gave you, with the blade exposed. You sat there rocking, thinking the time had finally come for you to see if God was real. You wanted to be seen, yet invisible, because you were not quite sure if you could bear witness to the entirety of yourself without certain dissolution. You knew for certain, that if you disrobed, and let go of the performance manliness mandated to you—if you were *your* self—and were rejection even more by those that *loved* you, you might not recover on earth, heaven or hell. You sat there rocking, pondering your life, wondering if it were possible to smart and black and loved. You wondered if you had any value aside from creating and fixing problems. Things, bad things, seem to follow wherever you were. Your mother, destitute after your birth. Your grandmother, consigned to being a lifelong caregiver when you arrived, just as a her youngest child had left the nest. Your father, disappeared, unknown and when known—after a honeymoon week of father-son bonding—disappeared, your presence, you believed, through his marriage in disarray. Even your body had begun to self-destruct, just after you finally began to develop muscles and definition, your skin erupted in a cascade of fleshy mountains. It seems that God too was disturbed, perhaps dumbfounded, by your ability to sew discord. Your first memories were of fond, special, unmentionable emotions toward men. But then he came, the one you loved, the one you shared a cradle with. He came, freckled, brown and smiling. He hugged you, 15 too, with a kiss on the head and a smiling face with wet eyes. He slyly took your knife and placed it to his own neck, before throwing it to the ground, remind you of your pack to live and die, together, forever. You laugh and smile and weep. You recalled, just last week this very maneuver. Your roles had been reversed. He was attempting to cut, you came to cauterize and hold. It's a wonder. You both felt and wielded the blade in a room of loud of people, invisible to all, but the brother from another's flesh. He saw you, so that you might. You will be seen. Don't fear the light.

But do study and run. Study the way men look at you and interact with your sisters. Know that you are not imprisoned by their rule, their rules or their imagined powers. Let your hair flow thick and curly, resistant of rules and decorum. Arch your eyebrows. Sashay your hips. Pectorals bulging, abs tight, continue to flex in your so-called wife beater and worry not about fitting in, but the joyous prospect of busting out. Remember that maleness is a construct, not a fulcrum, of this life. Break free early and often. Keep your sensitive side alive, he'll save you more than you'll ever know. Never stop writing, lest you forget what you've lived through. Love hard, love often and always tell yourself the truth. One day your words will save lives, beginning with you. Your voice will fill rooms, rallies and boom through auditoriums. Take this moment to live honestly, so that you might have something pure and true and soothing to say. Someone might just be listening, or reading.

Dearest Brother Outsider 25,

It's been nearly a year since you have turned 25. This age is pivotal for many, but even more-so for you, yet you decided to stay home, alone and celebrate with a full bottle of merlot. There was a possibility you wouldn't live until 15, you did that, but you never imagined to make it to 25. So many of your friends, cousins and acquaintances have died in one way or another. Many sit in the tombs of those gone to glory, but countless more are rotting away in bodies that serve as corporeal prisons: lifeless survivors of capitalisms, black neoliberalism, in/externalized anti-black-ness and empty promises of love, home and justice. Yet here you are, alive and somewhere near free. Still though, you struggle to see that freedom, struggle to define what it is, for you and whether that definition is real and true. You wonder whether anything is right or true. In your quest for free-dom no, liberation, you have become a wanderlust, post-structuralist of sorts. Can your own mind be trusted or is it endemically poisoned by the epistemologies of power accumulation? Do you own it? Perhaps it is sim-ply leased and your "critical" thoughts merely till within the limits of a permissible consciousness.

And what of love, honey? What of your practice of love? This year has been a milestone of sorts. You managed to date the same boy five times, over eleven months, with different names and let "the one" slip away. Surely, this isn't what Oprah meant when she admonished the world to live their best lives! None-the-less through it all, you garnered a deeper practice of self-love, a critical love ethic based in liberation and humanization. You have learned to see, while being seen, instead of scene. You have experienced the power of being held freely and not owned. You now know the differences and interlinkages between sex and love production. You have become a skilled pedagogue in the art of sexual diplomacy and fluent in the language of vulnerable, unflinching love—love that bids you good-night and greets you with butterflies before the sun announces its presence. You are present. You have learned to live.

Still living has its limits, beloved. Just three weeks ago, one of your younger brothers was shot in the hand, and you learned of it on Facebook. This functioned as a cold reminder of the distance between self and family—despite never growing up with this half-brother—that seems insurmountable. Is this, perhaps the difference between living and existing, or surviving and thriving? You wonder still, whether it was all worth it. Perhaps, if you would have gone to live with your father, instead of to some prestigious castle in New Mexico, you could've provided mentor-ship that may have changed the course of his life. Of course, that would've likely lead to another fight with your *father* about his homoantagonisms and heterosexual anxiety. You could only protect yourself with a hot-iron for so long. He might one day close around your throat when the iron is cold, or worse, out of reach. But you wonder still, was your education worth it? Did you mortgage the future of your siblings to attend white and racially unaware institutions like Tufts? While the school used your black body as an authenticator and credit card for its purchase of diversity points —using your likeness, your grade-dropping protests and demands for pro-

225

grams and research centers that center your history and present, on a former plantation—your brothers and sisters were stewing in the smog of a racial reality that was known but unspeakable. You know some things just are. They cannot be spoken. These things cannot be said because to speak of them is to conjure the truth of our destitute reality, our implicit, passive endorsement of subjugation and the hopelessness of it all. I'm convinced if black folks and BlaQueer folks and Latinx folks told each other the truth —at home, school, church, dinner, the club and while fucking—the nation might survive in its current character. If we were real, if we kept it 100, about our role in the communal raping we endure, the rupture we be swift, long and unforgiving. We would lose the identities we have built up as perpetual warriors in an unwinnable struggle. We would be forced to confront each and every sellout-ass move we have made in the name of survival, each time we have refinanced the lives of our peoples, of our parents, of our siblings, cousin and skinfolk. We would be forced to reckon with the votes we have cast—in blood, coin and ballot—for neoliberal black and so-called pro-black leaders, thinkers, artists, pastors and elected officials. Barack, Bill & Hillary would no longer be inspirational, nor would they be enough. We would have to re-examine and reconceive of the call to "love and protect each other." We would be forced to create and note the corollary to the blood-wrought cry of #BlackLivesMatter; we then began to chant and practice and teach and work and love and fight and cry and rejoice and create and rear and vote and pray and fuck and think and rest as if BLACK LIVES MATTER...OR ELSE.

This collection of writing provides one-hundred-sixty odd pages of your overcoming, your unbecoming and your re-membering, yet still and you look toward tomorrow: but you are no longer running away from to-day. Baby steps, I suppose. On the last days of 25, you are called to not only reconnect with and piece together and re-member the circumcised pieces of yourself, but that union between yourself and community, be-tween self and the choices deemed necessary to succeed, between self and critical and examination of the great beyond, between self and power and healing and love and justice and momma'em. It is true that black men lov-ing black men is a revolutionary act, but black people loving black people building loving, redemptive, healing, holistic communities and community practices is surely a practice of liberatory, divine homecoming. We have noted the Godless Circumcisions of our existences but now is the time to prepare, make way and midwife a season and practice of Cosmic Recon-ciliations. Remember this, beloved, we have nothing to lose but our chains.

Signed,

Tabias Olajuawon Wilson
Another Brother Gasping For Air

Brief Notes On Modern Warfare

HIV Criminalization, Black Bodies & The Noose That Won't Stop Swingin'

Black Flesh, Red Blood, White Law: The Criminalization of Black Sexualities

This piece originally appeared on TheBody.com in their series "Views On The Trial and Conviction of Michael Johnson, A Black Life That Matters." HIV continues to become a tool for the further criminalization of black persons. The urgency of the issue is compounded by countless data. However, nothing has been more illuminating than the unjust prosecution of Michael Johnson.

HIV criminalization laws codify significant hostility toward HIV-positive individuals, particularly those of color. At first glance, this is problematic because it creates a viral underclass. However, when put in the context of the persistent nature of racism and anti-blackness within the law and extra-judicial practices such as lynching, we can see how HIV criminalization also serves to compound oppression.

HIV-positive black men are targeted on the basis of their race and non-whiteness, as well as their health status as HIV positive. Our status as men who have sex with men, in addition to being black, hollows out a special place for us as sexual deviants and enemies of a white, patriarchal system that provides for and necessitates male sexual domination over women. Our sexualities complicate the stereotypes ascribed to black men (assumed to be straight) as hyper-sexual beings whose existence is a threat to the sexual power of white men and the inherent innocence of (white) women.

 Our lives challenge the traditional nature of the American sociopolitical landscape whereby men are formed, molded and reshaped as all-powerful beings who exist to provide and protect for women, particularly white women. As men who have same-sex attractions, our existence not only complicates and problematizes this narrative. We disrupt the historical reasoning that black men desire two things above all: 1) white, heterosexual masculinity and 2) to rape white women.

In the event that black men disavow these yearnings or disprove their existence -- in the case of Michael Johnson, for example -- it is read as an assault on whiteness as well as the benefits and privileges that this narrative provides for white and whitened individuals. This rejection of the ideology of white supremacy also removes the so-called "moral authority" that whites have clung to for the logical basis of the legal and extralegal apparatus in the U.S. This logic has been made clear in different eras, from the defense of lynching executed by white men and women to their silence in the sexual violence visited upon black women and men.

Lynchings were the result of allegations of rape by white women and/or sexual insubordination by black men. They functioned as disciplinary proceedings for black people who dared not offer their flesh in the manner, condition and speed accustomed to their white desirers. This is reminiscent of Johnson's criminal prosecution, where one accuser filed charges after noting how he wanted condomless sex because Michael was "huge" and only his "third black guy." These charges are seemingly not about harm, but about the right to enjoy a particular experience, a controlled experience, with a "huge" black penis. The alleged revelation of Johnson's HIV status robbed the accuser of power, a fond sexual memory and a particular, controlled eroticized, racial-sexual experience.

Lynchings were often marked by penectomy -- surgical removal of the penis -- with the images of the act widely displayed through official postcards, "art" and posters as travelling reminders or public service announcements. These public displays of terrorism, in circus form before thousands, worked to normalize and engrain images of the black body as inherently criminal and dangerous, and in need of control. This is not dissimilar to marking of many sexually active HIV survivors as "AIDS Monsters," legal pariahs and the most ardent enemies of the state (i.e., sex offenders, bioterrorists, attempted murders) while their faces are splayed across television screens and posters, and their bodies are subjected to a lifetime of state surveillance -- a social penectomy. The relationship between lynching and blackness, given that only black people were lynched, also served to reify the notion that white (and assumed heterosexual) sexualities and masculinities were the only socially and legally acceptable options.

Ida. B. Wells bravely, and courageously, led anti-lynching campaigns that articulated the linkages between fear and control of the black body with anxieties and white supremacy. She understood that lynching was not about solving the issue of gendered sexual violence -- otherwise white men would be routinely lynched for the raping of black and white women alike -- but instead about a system of racial-sexual domination, where some are killed for simply surviving and others are exalted for violent expressions of power and desire. We must urge organizers, advocates, courts and politicians to recognize an innate right to bodily autonomy and human dignity. In such a reality, no one would be unfairly penalized or ostracized for the contents of their blood. Instead, all would be implored to enhance the potential of our character by maximizing health, minimizing risks and congratulating each other on the daily act of survival.

EPILOGUE

I Saw Langston At The Altar, And Other BlaQueer Dreams

I wanted to be like Langston, social, observant and classy on the epidermis but as I grow older, Baldwin, Essex & Hemphill take root thru solitude, sex and drink in thru the mourning.

Dry tears and moist sunrises, comfort was found in full glasses in high rises, with few family around. Warmth, singing songs with tongues untied, not of Amerikkka but a world uncompromised, by the truth of black hips spread wide by wet tongues, wide fingers and Mandingos appetites..unrelenting sex, power, positivity and holy wholeness, prostrate on the Altar of the undying.

We grew strong in the kitchen, not as spectators, but as surveyors of power, revolutionaries, testators. We left bones on the floor, of the houses always ours, for hours we burned them like the sage of our foremothers.

Langston lay low, code switching with brilliance. Saved many lives with years of resilience. The power of a pen to tell two stories at once: one a yellow negro tamed with no wants, another a calm nigga, clever and willing–to tell the truth about white folks while also fulfilling, the hope of other brothers, spirits unbroken, but he spoke in the dark until we children awoken.

Baldwin came next, with a tongue of hell fire. Infernos in our bellies did that homo negro inspire. His tongue spoke no codes, no apologies, just black. Told whitey, Elijah and Martin they whack. He wrote of a blackness that had sex so freely, unless you were a woman, well then his tongue got real squeaky. He spoke of black girls with black eyes, as if he had no clue of the terror in the skies..raped, beaten and cast out as hoes by whitey and Malcolm and all manner of bros.

In comes old Essex, with an intersectional view. Demilitarize the body and take this in too, I'm black, queer, poz and sexy and don't you want me too? The secret of fear, is that it's cloaked in desire. You call war on my body because it's no longer yours sire! We may talk about coin, perhaps it's for hire, but make no mistake, it's still about desire. Put your ring on my cock, or in her vagina, our love needs no permission from the U.S. state nor its extrajudical arms. Kill us all now, let this damn virus spread, but just know this shug, I'll never be dead. We live in the cosmos and the canals of your spirit. Just listen closely and I'm sure you will hear it. I am you and you are me, 300 years later and you're drawn back to me. Black like the universe you fall to my pull, gravity didn't send you, you're just race's fool. Sweet dreams old Judy, we bid you Adeu, but no more code switching, it's so 82.

Langston, Baldwin and Essex—along with Joseph Beam, Marlon Riggs, Rotemi Fani Kayode and Audre Lorde—are just a sampling of the known BlaQueer people that have come before me, before us, clearing the way for our essence. They shed tears, shed flesh and shed dreams so that they might survive and one of us, if not all of us, might have the liberation that so often eluded them. Within each of these ancestors is a fire that cannot be dampened. It is a call to live: better, freerer and more lovingly. This call to live lovingly is not simply one of self-care or romantic trysts but a call to recognize the ways in which we see, are seen and interact with one another. We are called to change the equation for humanization. Vulnerability among us cannot be a signifier for vultures, parasites or scavengers to pick at those exposed pieces of us. No, instead, it should be a clarion call to the griots, the healers, the shamans, the artists, the children, the elders, the lovers and all those with a beating heart to come and gather'round: so that they too may assist in, and experience, the love practice of a village without bounds.

Godless Circumcisions is not a collection of fairy tales or a tome of trauma. It is a documentation of the myriad ways our bodies and souls are cleaved and clawed at, branded and dismembered, sold and erased. It is a call to re-call, re-member and recollect those pieces of us that have never been deemed as convenient to the projects of capitalism, imperialism, racisms, nativism, cisheteropatriarchy, consumerism, ableism, masculinities or the American Daydream. It is a call for us to wakeup—not bearing arms of short-lived rage but that of a critical love ethic—so that we may not only destroy, in order to rebuild, but become architects that construct beyond old and next anxieties. Our time has been, and always will be, now. We have nothing to lose but our chains. We must love and protect each other, always. If we do not arise to the ongoing challenge of anti-black genocides, we will soon be forced to face the corollary to Black Lives Matter: Or Else. The next time burned folks, lashed folks, black and other colored folks, capitalist-fucked-white folks rise; it won't be another blowhard speech on Washington. No, it will be Fanon's Prophecy greeting us at our work place, our favorite parks and at our dinner tables. The R/ Evolution will take your children.